Frommer's®

24

GREAT

walking

TOURS IN

LONDON

WILEY

Wiley Publishing, Inc.

Author: Richard Jones
Managing Editor: Paul Mitchell
Series Editor: Donna Wood
Art Editor: Alison Fenton
Page layout: Andrew Milne
Copy Editor: Sharon Amos
Proofreader: Joey Clarke
Cartography provided by the Mapping Services
Department of AA Publishing
Production: Stephanie Allen

Edited, designed and produced by AA Publishing.
© Automobile Association Developments Limited 2008

Published by AA Publishing.

Published in the United States by
Wiley Publishing, Inc.
111 River Street, Hoboken, NJ 07030

Find us online at Frommers.com

Frommer's is a registered trademark of Arthur Frommer.
Used under license.

  This product includes mapping
data licensed from the Ordnance
Survey ® with the permission of the Controller of Her
Majesty's Stationery Office. © Crown copyright 2008.
All rights reserved. Licence number 100021153.

ISBN 978-0-470-22895-1

A03326

A CIP catalogue record for this book is available from the
British Library.

The contents of this publication are believed correct
at the time of printing. Nevertheless, the publishers
cannot accept responsibility for errors or omissions,
or for changes in details given in this guide or for
the consequences of any reliance on the information
provided by the same. Assessments of attractions and
so forth are based upon the author's own experience
and, therefore, descriptions given in this guide necessarily
contain an element of subjective opinion which may not
reflect the publishers' opinion or dictate a reader's own
experiences on another occasion.

Colour reproduction by Keene Group, Andover
Printed in China by Leo Paper Group

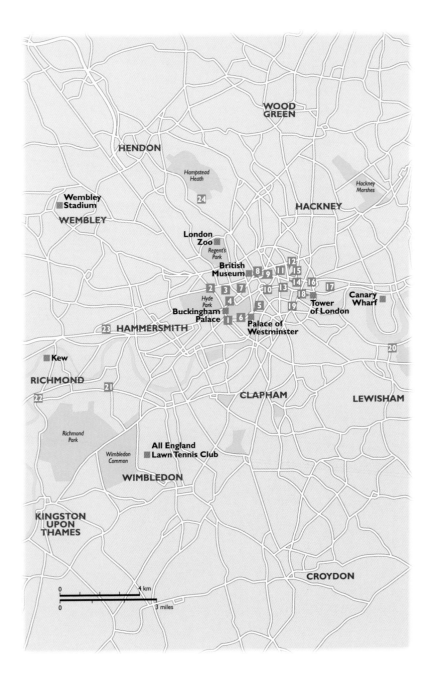

WOOD
GREEN

HENDON

Hampstead
Heath

Hackney
Marshes

Wembley
■ Stadium

HACKNEY

WEMBLEY

London
■ Zoo

Regent's
Park

British
Museum ■

8 9 11

12
15

24

2

3 7

14 16

17

10 13

18

Hyde
Park

4

Canary
Wharf ■

Buckingham
Palace ■

5

19

Tower
of London

1 6

■ Kew

Palace of
Westminster

23 HAMMERSMITH

20

RICHMOND

21

22

CLAPHAM

LEWISHAM

Richmond
Park

All England
■ Lawn Tennis Club

Wimbledon
Common

WIMBLEDON

KINGSTON
UPON
THAMES

CROYDON

0   4 km

0   3 miles

CONTENTS

Introduction   6

1   Knockings in Belgravia   8
2   Hangings and Hoaxes   14
3   Spectres and Super Sleuths   22
4   Spies and Spooks in Mayfair   28
5   Wandering in Westminster   36
6   A Brush with Royalty   42
7   Ghosts and Greasepaint   50
8   Museums and the Macabre   56
9   Curses in Covent Garden   64
10   Ghosts by Gaslight   70
11   Monks, Murder and Masons   78
12   Burnings and Bodysnatchers   84
13   The Splendour of St Paul's   92
14   Ghosts of the Old City   98
15   Remnants of Rome   106
16   Jack the Ripper's Trail   112
17   Lore and Legend in Wapping   120
18   Wanderings and Wizards   126
19   Bards and Bawds in Southwark   134
20   Shipshape in Greenwich   140
21   Hauntings of Barnes Common   148
22   Murder in Richmond   154
23   The Chilling Streets of Chiswick   162
24   Mystery in Hampstead   168

Index   174
Acknowledgements   176

Introduction

The streets of London are steeped in history, and the best way to discover what they have to offer is on foot. Walking helps you to make sense of the great sprawl that is Britain's capital. It enables you to get beneath its skin and discover the vivid history, diversity of cultures, and the modern verve that are London's lifeblood.

Like Rome, London wasn't built in a day, but has grown and evolved over the past 2,000 years. From a central axis around St Paul's and the Tower of London, it has expanded outwards, absorbing what were once remote villages into its urban landscape, and obliterating ancient woods and marshlands. Yet, in so doing, it has allowed little bits of those places to survive, and for those who are willing to scratch the surface and explore away from the busy modern streets, a rich and rewarding experience awaits.

In this book you will find 24 walks that capture the essence of London. They take in well-known tourist attractions but also include secret places that the rush of modern London has yet to engulf. Several of the walks explore the hidden alleyways and ancient courtyards that people who work in the centre of London pass on a daily basis and yet remain oblivious to. Others provide real contrasts. One moment you might be pushing against the seething mass of humanity that teems along Oxford Street and around Piccadilly Circus, the next you have ducked down a passageway to find yourself blinking in disbelief at picturesque mews, grand squares and magnificent houses.

London comprises a much larger canvas than the well-known neighbourhoods of the City and Westminster. It is made up of lots of villages strung together around the central core. This book gives you the opportunity to venture to these outlying places. You will stroll through the leafy streets of Hampstead and hear tales of ghosts on the wilder reaches of its justifiably famous heath. You will climb the hills of royal Richmond to gaze out at some of the most amazing views imaginable. You will wander the paths that snake across Barnes Common, once a wild and remote location and a favoured haunt of highwaymen such as Dick Turpin. Graveyards and burial grounds abound, as do tales of ghosts and murders. You will walk in the footsteps of the famous and forgotten, and will gain an insight into the events and characters that have helped shape London.

But the walks are not just about events and people. Each one has been paced out to ensure that it blends intriguing sites and sights with a route that is as atmospheric as it is fascinating. Limited space has meant that not every point of interest – in a city that abounds in them – could be included. But you will most certainly encounter them. You'll spot wall plaques to people who, in one way or another, have contributed to the rich diversity of London, and come across statues of important figures from the city's fascinating past. Dark alleyways that you might otherwise have avoided become doorways of discovery through which you find hidden gems from bygone ages.

So be sure to take your time. Explore every twist and turn and absorb the ambience of the many different neighbourhoods. But above all else, enjoy the histories and ponder the mysteries that have, literally, been written in the streets you're walking.

Knockings in Belgravia

Belgravia is one of London's most fashionable areas. Its tall terraces of gleaming white houses recall a bygone age when 'class' was everything.

This walk will take you through some of the most splendid streets of Belgravia, with the opportunity to explore some of its hidden backwaters. It will also introduce you to the more sordid aspects of this world of plenty. These include the infamous 1974 murder of the family nanny by Lord Lucan, a crime that led to one of the greatest mysteries of the late 20th century. You will also see the house in which the Beatles' manager, Brian Epstein, hosted some of the most lavish showbiz parties of the mid 1960s, but where in 1967 he lost the battle with his own personal demons. A highlight of the walk is the opportunity to attend a sitting at the elegant headquarters of the Spiritualist Association, while a visit to a lovely hidden and haunted pub, in a delightful but hard-to-find mews, makes a fitting finale. All in all, this walk is a worthwhile introduction to a lesser known part of London where a combination of history and mystery should keep you wondering what the next corner turned might reveal.

From the Shakespeare pub at Victoria Station, cross over Buckingham Palace Road via the crossing. Bear left, keep ahead over Grosvenor Gardens, go first right into Lower Belgrave Street, then left into Ebury Street.

At No. 22 on the right there is a plaque to Ian Fleming, creator of James Bond, who lived at 22B from 1936 to 1939. The building's odd appearance – it used to be a 19th-century chapel – appealed to Fleming, and the fact that it was reputedly haunted proved an added attraction. He turned it into a suitably avant-garde bachelor pad in which he pursued his hobbies: collecting first editions and surrealist art, seducing women, gambling and gourmandizing.

2 Backtrack along this left side of Ebury Street and go left into Lower Belgrave Street. Cross to its right side and pause outside the Plumber's Arms, which dates from the 1820s.

On the night of 7 November 1974, at 9.45pm, a bloodstained woman burst into the bar of this pub and screamed: "Help me… I've just escaped from being murdered. He's in the house. He's murdered the nanny!" She was the Countess of Lucan, and she had just fled her nearby home, leaving her three children behind. On the walls of the pub you can read yellowed newspaper articles detailing its involvement in those early moments of what would become one of the great mysteries of the late 20th century, the disappearance of Richard John Bingham, seventh Earl of Lucan.

WHERE TO EAT

🍴 THE HORSE AND GROOM,
7 Groom Place;
Tel: 020 7235 6980.
www.horseandgroom.net
Hidden away in quiet mews, this intimate pub has the feeling of a friendly country local.

🍴 THE SPIRITUALIST ASSOCIATION OF GREAT BRITAIN,
33 Belgrave Square;
Tel: 020 7235 3351.
Mostly drinks and snacks from machines but with a tranquil rear yard where you can sit outside and absorb the ambience.

🍴 THE GRENADIER,
18 Wilton Row;
Tel: 020 7235 3074.
Friendly local boozer.

3 Continue along Lower Belgrave Street and pause outside No. 46.

This was the house from which Lady Lucan had escaped her attacker. When the police arrived, they forced open the front door and found the children unharmed in their bedrooms. But in the basement they found a pool of blood on the floor and inside a bloodstained sack they discovered the battered body of the Lucans' nanny, Sandra Rivett. Lady Lucan subsequently claimed that her estranged husband had murdered the nanny and then begun to attack her.

DISTANCE **2 miles (3.2km)**

ALLOW **2 hours**

START **Terminus Place in the forecourt of Victoria Station**

FINISH **Hyde Park Underground Station**

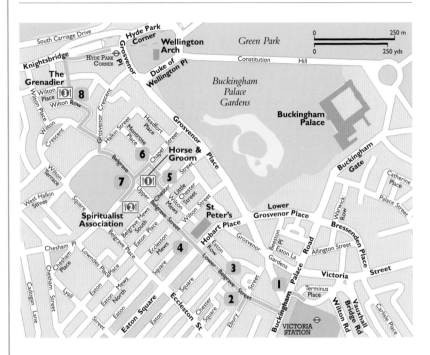

Later that night Lord Lucan arrived at a friend's house and claimed that as he was passing No. 46 he had seen his wife being attacked by an intruder. Rushing to assist, he had slipped over in a pool of blood and the stranger ran off. He then tried to calm his wife but she ran into the street crying: "Murder!" This, he claimed, caused him to panic, and he fled the scene. After that night Lord Lucan was never seen again and various theories have been put forward to explain his fate – which still remains unknown despite

numerous reported sightings of him all over the world.

4 Continue into Eaton Square. Keep ahead over Hobart Place, passing St Peter's Church on the right, which, if open, is worth a visit. Go over Wilton Street into Upper Belgrave Street. Turn right into Chester Street and take the first left into Groom Place.

You suddenly find yourself in a pre-car age of picturesque mews properties

that were once the living quarters for the coachmen who attended the grand houses of Belgravia. The ground-level double doors gave access to the stables where the horses and coaches were kept, while the coachmen and their families lived in the rooms above. Today, just one of these properties would probably cost the combined wages of several lifetimes for every 19th-century coachman in the whole of Belgravia.

5 Turn right in front of the Horse and Groom pub, take the next turning left, walk up the incline and go right into Chapel Street. Immediately on the right you will see No. 24.

In December 1964 Brian Epstein, the manager who had steered the Beatles to worldwide fame and universal acclaim, bought this house. He hosted many memorable showbiz parties here including, on 19 May 1967, the launch for the Beatles' upcoming groundbreaking album *Sgt Pepper's Lonely Hearts Club Band*. The Beatles attended and posed for photographs on the doorstep. However, Epstein was finding the pressure of managing the world's first supergroup and the stress of coming to terms with his homosexuality unbearable, and had begun a drink- and pills-fuelled downward spiral. He was found dead in his bedroom here on 22 August 1967,

the victim of an overdose. A verdict of accidental death was recorded, although some suggested suicide or even murder.

6 Proceed over Groom Place, walk along Chapel Street and, as it veers left, cross Upper Belgrave Street. Keep ahead into Belgrave Square. A few doors along is No. 33, the headquarters of the Spiritualist Association of Great Britain.

The Spiritualist Association bought this building in 1955 and it was opened by Air Chief Marshal Lord Dowding, a fervent Spiritualist, who also took part in an 'At Home' to help raise much-needed finance for the new headquarters. Visitors are welcome to attend daily séances here, as well as witnessing public demonstrations of clairvoyance. One of the Association's most treasured possessions is the chair in which Sir Arthur Conan Doyle (1859-1930), another committed Spiritualist, wrote many of his popular Sherlock Holmes detective stories. The building has a wonderfully tranquil ambience and provides a welcome respite from the rush of modern London.

SPIRITUALIST ASSOCIATION;

OPEN DAILY www.sagb.org.uk

7 Backtrack and proceed counter-clockwise around Belgrave Square. Go over Halkin Street, pass to the right of the statue of Sir Robert Grosvenor, the first Marquess of Westminster, and keep ahead to enter Wilton Crescent. Turn first right into Wilton Row. As this road bears left it becomes almost rural

in character. Along on the right you will find one of the smallest and most atmospheric pubs in London.

The Grenadier is patriotically painted red, white and blue. A red sentry box outside; swords, bayonets and other military memorabilia inside recall the days when this was, reputedly, the officers' mess for the Duke of Wellington's regiment. It is said to be haunted by the ghost of a young subaltern caught cheating at cards, who either killed himself in shame or was flogged to death by his brother officers.

8 Go left out of the Grenadier and through the red gate immediately on your left into Old Barrack Yard. On the right is the stone horse mount from Wellington's day, said to have been used by the Iron Duke himself. Keep ahead past the tiny cottages, proceed through the arched passage, turn left and follow the path right through the modern concrete jungle that springs up around you. Go right along Knightsbridge and keep going until you arrive at Hyde Park Underground Station.

Hangings and Hoaxes

In the mews and streets behind Oxford Street, London's most popular shopping destination, you'll encounter all kinds of unexpected goings-on.

Beginning alongside Marble Arch on what is one of the busiest traffic islands in London, you might be forgiven for thinking the roar of cars and buses will be your constant companion. But worry not. Within a few minutes you will have stepped into a pleasant mews behind Park Lane and be searching the dark windows of a baroque-looking building for a glimpse of the ghost of one of the most famous royal mistresses of all time. You momentarily encounter the traffic of Oxford Street, but soon venture into a delightful warren of pretty mews, far removed from the urban rush. Having admired the house where 19th-century novelist Wilkie Collins was living when he wrote the first English detective story, you visit the place where the man behind one of the 19th century's greatest scams died. The grand finale occurs in yet another quiet mews where in 1820 the Cato Street conspiracy reached its bloody conclusion.

| Leave Hyde Park station by following the signs towards exit 7. Follow the tunnel as it bears right and go up the stairs of exit 3 on the left.

To your right is Marble Arch, designed in 1827 by John Nash. It used to stand in front of Buckingham Palace but was moved to its present location in 1851. A full history of it and of the surrounding area can be read on the board to the left of the exit.

From the 14th to the 18th century thousands of people flocked to this area, then known as Tyburn Road, to enjoy the spectacle of public executions. The gallows used to be situated on the Edgware Road, to the left of the Odeon Cinema behind Marble Arch. When the bodies were cut down after a hanging the crowd would surge forward to touch them in the belief that they held medicinal properties.

2 Backtrack down the stairs of exit 3, go left towards exits 4-7, then follow the sign for exits 5-7 and as you bear left, keep ahead into exit 6 marked Park Lane East Side. Go left up the stairs and first left into Wood's Mews. Turn left into Dunraven Street, keep ahead over Green Street and pause outside No. 19 on the right.

This exuberant baroque-looking building dates from the 1890s but stands on the site of the house of Lillie Langtry, society beauty and semi-official mistress of the Prince of Wales, later King Edward VII.

Her ghost is said to wander inside the current building, as do the ghosts of at least two headless men and several victims of the hangings at nearby Tyburn!

3 Go next right on to North Row. Stop a little way along on the right outside North Row Buildings, erected in 1888 by the St George's Workmen's Model Dwellings Association.

The architect of these buildings, Robert Henry Burden, had designed many workhouses, and his initial plans were for much taller buildings. But the owners of the grand houses on Hereford Street, whose gardens the dwellings overlooked, became alarmed at the thought of the working classes looking down on them and complained to the Duke of Westminster. As a result, the height of the dwellings was reduced to a more socially acceptable level.

4 Go next left on to Park Street and fight your way through the seething masses to cross Oxford Street via the traffic lights and keep ahead into Portman Street. Pause at its junction with Bryanston Street.

The building on the opposite side was once the Spencer Hotel. On 14 March 1922, 65-year-old Lady White was found dying from head wounds on her bed in the hotel. Since there were no signs of forced entry the police concluded that the killer was connected to the hotel and began interviewing the staff. They became suspicious of 18-year-old pantry

DISTANCE 3 miles (4.8km)

ALLOW I hour 45 minutes

START Marble Arch Underground Station, Hyde Park Exit 3

FINISH Edgware Road Underground Station

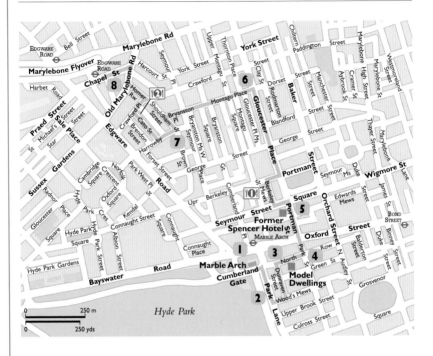

boy Henry Jacoby and, on searching him, found two bloodstained handkerchiefs. He confessed that he had intended to rob a guest's room and had taken a hammer with him to use 'if necessary'. He found the door to Lady White's room unlocked and entered. She had woken up and he had beaten her to stop her raising the alarm. Despite a public outcry for leniency, Jacoby was hanged for his crime.

5 Keep ahead along Portman Street, turn left into Seymour Street and go

first right into Berkeley Mews. Go right on to Upper Berkeley Street then left along Gloucester Place. Keep ahead over George Street and pause outside No. 65.

William Wilkie Collins lived here from September 1867 until February 1888. Throughout the 1860s, Collins had been suffering with a condition known as rheumatic gout and took ever-increasing doses of laudanum to ease the pain. This led to paranoid delusions and he became convinced that he was always

accompanied by a doppelgänger, which he named Ghost Wilkie. While living here, his book *The Moonstone* – now considered the first English detective novel and a book that helped establish crime fiction as a genre – was published. The effects of opium addiction are dealt with in *The Moonstone* and Collins later claimed that such was his consumption of laudanum that he had no memory of writing large sections of it.

6 Go next left into Montagu Place and over Montagu and Bryanston Squares into Bryanston Place. Keep ahead over Seymour Place then cross over Shouldham Street to No. 21.

It was here on 1 April 1898 that Arthur Orton died. Twenty-five years earlier Orton, a sheep slaughterer from Australia, had attempted to pull off a gigantic hoax by claiming to be Roger Tichborne, wealthy landowner and heir to a baronetcy, whose ship had disappeared on a voyage between Brazil and Jamaica. Lady Tichborne had refused to believe her son was dead and offered a reward in Australian newspapers for any word of him. Orton responded with a letter in which he addressed her as 'My dear Mother', and the hoax was under way. Lady Tichborne met him in Paris in 1866, accepted him as her son, paid off his debts and afforded him an annual

allowance of £1,000. But his claims were disputed by other members of the family and, after what was (at the time) the longest-running case in the history of Britain's criminal and civil courts, he was sentenced to 14 years in prison. His last years at this house were spent in dire poverty. Yet such was the legend of the Tichborne Claimant that 5,000 people lined the Edgware Road to watch his body being taken to a pauper's grave in Paddington cemetery.

7 Continue left along Shouldham Street, go right on to Harrowby Street, keep ahead over Molyneux Street and once past No. 47, go right through the covered passageway into Cato Street. Walk its length and, on the left at its far side, pause outside the red door of No. 1a.

The building has hardly changed since 23 February 1820 when it was the scene of what the *Morning Chronicle* described as 'DREADFUL RIOT AND MURDER'. It was in an upstairs room over what was then a cowshed that a group of about 20 politically malcontented young men, headed by Arthur Thistlewood, had gathered to put the finishing touches to a plot to assassinate the entire British Cabinet, who would be dining at nearby Grosvenor Square later that night. Unbeknown to the conspirators, their gang had been infiltrated by a police spy and, as they began their preparations, a party of Bow Street Runners burst in on them with a cry of "We are police officers, lay down your arms."

WHERE TO EAT

🍽 **THE BRICKLAYER'S ARMS,**
6 New Quebec Street;
Tel: 020 7724 9949.
You pass the back of this unassuming little pub as you head through Berkeley Mews. Standard pub fare.

🍽 **THE WINDSOR CASTLE,**
27-29 Crawford Place;
Tel: 020 7723 4371.
This curious little pub has a full-sized guard box outside and every inch of inner space is covered with royal crests, flags, coins and statuettes, not to mention signed photographs of numerous celebrities. Expect basic pub grub.

One of the officers, Richard Smithers, moved forward to make the arrests, but Thistlewood raised his sword and ran him through with it. "Oh my God, I am done!" Smithers cried out, before falling down dead. Thistlewood managed to escape but he was captured the next day and on 1 May 1820 he and four other of the conspirators were executed at Newgate Prison.

8 Pass under the next covered passageway and go right on to Crawford Place, left into Homer Row, right on to Old Marylebone Road, then first left into Chapel Street. A little way along Chapel Street, on the right, is Edgware Road Underground Station where this walk ends.

Spectres and Super Sleuths

A walk for those who have thrilled at the stories of Sherlock Holmes, and who also like their sightseeing to be tinged with scandal and the bizarre.

The walk begins with a visit to the house where the composer Handel (1685-1759) lived and died – the same house where Jimi Hendrix experienced ghostly sightings in the 1960s. From here you will venture into a wonderful neighbourhood of grand houses and hidden-away mews. You will stand outside the property where a young doctor by the name of Arthur Conan Doyle waited in vain for patients at his newly set-up surgery and wiled away the hours honing his Sherlock Holmes stories. Then you will delve into a mews where one of the greatest political scandals of the early 1960s, the Profumo affair, literally caught the government of the day with its trousers down. Via a decidedly creepy former burial ground, and a house in which it was widely believed the Messiah was going to be born in 1814, you take a stroll along Baker Street to stand on the site of 221b, perhaps one of the most famous fictional addresses in the world.

1 Bear right out of Bond Street underground exit, go over Davies Street to pass between the phone box and the mail box and keep ahead into South Molton Lane. Gray's Antique Market, to your right, is worth delving in to, to explore the stalls. Go over Brook Street and ahead into Avery Row. Just after Hardridge on the left, turn left into Lancashire Court. Turn left after No. 12, go down the cobbled ramp, through the brick arched passage and turn left at Jo Malone. Right is the Handel Museum.

George Frideric Handel (1685-1759) moved into this house in the summer of 1723 and lived here until his death in the upstairs bedroom 36 years later. In 2000, the building's upper storeys were leased to the Handel Trust, who set about turning it into the Handel Museum. During the restoration project there were reports of a ghostly female shape brushing past volunteers as they worked in the house. Since the appearances were often accompanied by the lingering smell of perfume, it was wondered if the haunting might be linked to either Faustina Bordoni or Francesca Cuzzoni, two sopranos who often visited Handel and who vied with each other to perform in his operas. The house next door, No. 23, is also part of the museum, and was the home of guitarist and rock legend Jimi Hendrix from 1968 to 1969. He too saw a ghost while living here.

HANDEL HOUSE MUSEUM;

www.handelhouse.org

GRAY'S ANTIQUES MARKET;

MON-FRI 10-6 www.grays.biz

2 Exit left from the house, go left up the cobbled ramp, right on to Brook Street then left along New Bond Street. Keep ahead over Blenheim Street, cross Oxford Street and keep ahead into Vere Street. Pretty St Peter's Church at the top on the right is worth a visit if open, and a brief history can be read on the outer wall. Go right along Henrietta Place and cross cautiously to its left side. Go left into Wimpole Street, keep ahead over Wigmore Street and cross to its right side. A little way along on the right, No. 6 has a blue plaque to Sir Frederick Treves (1853-1923), the doctor who befriended Joseph Merrick, the so-called Elephant Man. Keep going along Wimpole Street, go over Queen Anne Street and on arrival at the junction with New Cavendish Street go over the traffic lights, off which veer right and turn first left into Wimpole Mews. Towards its far end on the left, pause outside the brown door of No. 17.

DISTANCE 3.5 miles (5.6km)

ALLOW 2 hours

START Bond Street Underground Station, Davies Street Exit

FINISH Baker Street Underground Station

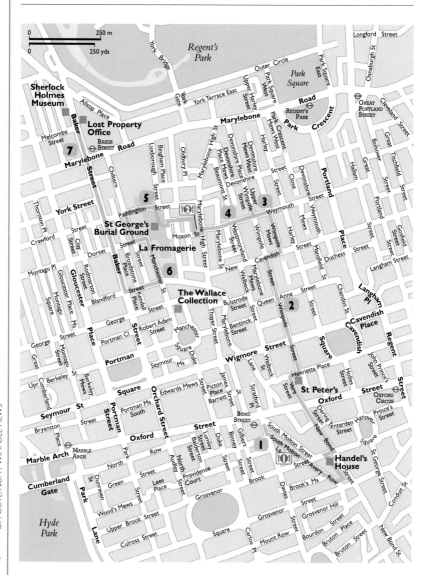

In 1963 this was the home of Dr Stephen Ward, an osteopath with a lucrative sideline in introducing wealthy and powerful men to pretty young women. The latter included 17-year-old Christine Keeler, who moved in with Ward and who was visited here separately by her lovers Eugene Ivanov, a Russian diplomat, and John Profumo, whose position as the English War Minister posed a potential security threat and resulted in the Profumo Scandal.

3 Keep ahead through Wimpole Mews, go left along Weymouth Street and first right into Upper Wimpole Street to pause outside No. 2 on the right.

Dr Arthur Conan Doyle (1859-1930) leased a consulting room here in 1891 and set himself up as an ophthalmologist. When the patients failed to materialize, he passed his days writing short stories about a character whom he had 'already handled in two little books'. That character was Sherlock Holmes and the short stories written here caught the public imagination and launched Conan Doyle on the road to literary fame and fortune, elevating his creation into the realm of sleuthing legends.

4 Backtrack to the lights and go right along Weymouth Street. Keep ahead over Beaumont Street and turn left on to Marylebone High Street. Go right along Moxon Street, first right into Garbutt Place, then left through Ossington Buildings, which date from

1888. The next section acquires a gloomy, almost sinister feel, lined as it is by tall buildings and even taller trees that cast the walkway into perpetual shadow. Turn left into Ashland Place and go right through the gates into Paddington Street Gardens. There is a history board immediately on the right as you enter.

These gardens have a macabre history. The site was founded in 1731 as St George's Burial Ground, an overflow graveyard for the local parish church. It closed in 1814, by which time 80,000 people had been buried here. It remains consecrated ground to this day. Turn right along the path and pause alongside the mausoleum erected by Richard Fitzpatrick to the memory of his wife Susanna, who died in 1759 aged 30. It is the only memorial to have survived in this section of the burial ground.

5 Go left by the mausoleum, keep ahead past the fountain, follow the path as it swings right and go out of the gate. Another section of the burial ground can be seen on the opposite side of the road. Turn left along Paddington Street, first left into Chiltern Street, left into Dorset Street and bend right into Manchester Street. Keep to the right side, noting the faces that look down on you from above the doors, and pause outside No. 38.

This nondescript building hardly looks like a suitable setting for the birth of the Messiah, yet that is exactly what was due to take place here on 19 October 1814. This auspicious event was eagerly awaited by the followers of the prophetess Joanna Southcott. As the date approached, shops did a roaring trade in cradles containing dolls representing Shiloh, the anticipated saviour. Statesmen and ambassadors came to visit the 64-year-old prophetess, as did 22 doctors, 17 of whom declared emphatically that she was indeed pregnant. When 19 October passed with no appearance of Shiloh, Joanna's followers continued their vigil by her bedside until she died at 3am on 28 December 1814. A subsequent autopsy revealed that internal flatulence, coupled with glandular enlargement of the breasts, had given the appearance of pregnancy.

6 Keep ahead along Manchester Street. The red-brick building you can see in the distance houses the Wallace Collection and is worth a detour. Otherwise, turn first right into Blandford Street. Keep ahead over Chiltern Street and go right along Baker Street. Walk its full length and go over Marylebone Road via the crossing to keep ahead into the continuation of Baker Street. Just past the London Transport Lost Property Office, go left over the crossing, veer right over Melcombe Street and pause outside the large building on the left.

This is one of the most famous fictional addresses in London: 221b Baker Street, the premises of Sherlock Holmes. It was formerly the Abbey National Building Society and such was the volume of

WHERE TO EAT

🍽 **VICTORY CAFE MILK BAR,**
South Molton Lane;
Tel: 020 7629 7034.
On the lower level of Gray's Antique Market. The decor is a real throwback to the days of rationing.

🍽 **LA FROMAGERIE,**
2-4 Moxon Street;
Tel: 020 7935 0341.
www.lafromagerie.co.uk
A specialist cheese shop with a café attached that provides mouthwatering meals.

correspondence that arrived here from all over the world addressed to Holmes that the society allocated a member of staff to act as Holmes's secretary with the duty of replying to each of the letters. At the time of writing, the building is being converted into luxury apartments. A few doors past it, on the left, is the Sherlock Holmes Museum, where you can step through the front door and be taken back to the consulting rooms of the world's most famous detective.

MUSEUM;
OPEN DAILY 9.30-6 www.sherlock-holmes.co.uk
WALLACE COLLECTION;
OPEN DAILY 10-5 www.wallacecollection.org

7 Exit right out of the museum and backtrack along this section of Baker Street. On the left you will see Baker Street Underground Station, where this walk ends.

Spies and Spooks in Mayfair

Mayfair is an area of contrasts. In some parts it has a sleepy, almost rural ambience; in others office blocks tower over noisy, traffic-clogged streets.

This walk avoids the modern-day clamour and concentrates instead on secret mews that lead to hidden courtyards where the charm and elegance of a bygone age hold sway. It is a tour to savour rather than rush. It begins on Piccadilly, perhaps one of the busiest roads in London. Yet within a short period you have stumbled into the lanes and passageways of Shepherd Market, a village-like gem. Blue plaques to famous – and not so famous – former residents abound, while hidden pubs offer havens in which to seek refreshment and refuge. Exquisite shops and breathtakingly ornate churches sit cheek by jowl with peaceful gardens. The area also once had associations with the twilight world of subterfuge and espionage, and part of the walk will take you into a delightful garden where Cold War spies once left secret messages for their handlers. As a finale, you find yourself outside what was once London's most haunted house to hear about the dreadful consequences of an encounter with its ghost.

From Green Park station go left along Stratton Street, right on to Piccadilly and keep ahead over Bolton, Clarges and Half Moon streets.

The blue plaque at No. 94 Piccadilly commemorates Lord Palmerston, who lived here from 1857 until his death at the grand old age of 81 in 1865. For many years the building was occupied by the Naval and Military Club, commonly known as the In and Out Club on account of the large black lettering on its gateposts, intended to guide cabbies in and out of the forecourt. The building was bombed in World War II and two members were killed. One of them, Major Henry Braddell, began to haunt the club dressed in smart military uniform and ankle-length greatcoat. Another phantom was said to appear suddenly, scare victims witless and then disappear. Many years ago a man went into convulsions and died of a seizure shortly after visiting the club. Speculation was rife that his fit had been brought on by an encounter with the ghost.

2 Go next right into White Horse Street. Walk its length and go left into Shepherd Market.

This is named after Edward Shepherd, the architect and builder responsible for many of Mayfair's properties. He reasoned that, although local households might buy their luxury items in Bond Street and Piccadilly, they would still need local shops for everyday staples such as milk, bread and meat. In 1735 he erected a market building on the site where the annual Mayfair, which gave its name to this area, had previously been held. Today this pedestrianized enclave remains the village heart of Mayfair and offers the casual stroller an eclectic and pleasant mix of wine bars, shops and a concentration of pubs where the servants of the great houses of Mayfair once gathered to enjoy their rare time off.

3 Go first right through the covered passageway; turn right on leaving, then left by Ye Grapes Pub. Turn left along Curzon Street, cross to its right side at the crossing and a little way along you'll find Crewe House.

This beautiful building, set well back in its own grounds, was built in 1730

DISTANCE **2 miles (3.2km)**

ALLOW **I hour 45 minutes**

START **Green Park Underground Station, Stratton Street Exit**

FINISH **Green Park Underground Station**

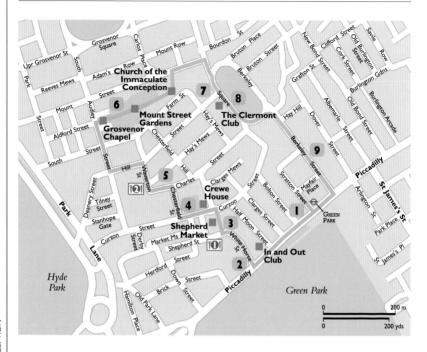

and was the home of Edward Shepherd. Much altered in the 19th century, it was purchased by the Marquess of Crewe in 1899 and renamed to commemorate his occupancy. It is one of the few surviving original grand Mayfair mansions and is today the embassy of Saudi Arabia.

4 Continue past Crewe House and turn first right into Chesterfield Street, the least altered of all Mayfair's Streets, with many of its houses surviving from the 18th century.

A plaque on the wall of No. 4 commemorates the residency of Beau Brummell, trendsetter and fashion icon of the Regency period.

5 Go left into Charles Street and keep ahead into Waverton Street. Bear right at The Red Lion then left along Hill Street. Turn right into South Audley Street, keep ahead over South Street, lined with exclusive shops. Pass through the portico of the Grosvenor Chapel and go immediately right into

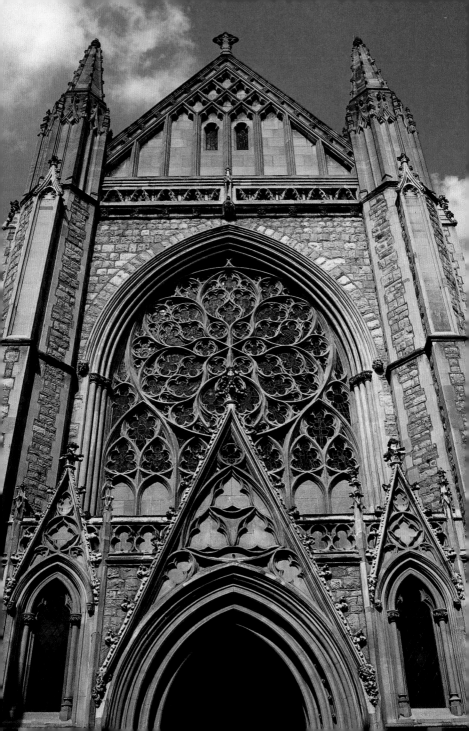

Chapel Place North. Keep ahead through the gate into Mount Street Garden.

This lovely garden was laid out in 1889 on a site formerly occupied by the burial ground of St George's Hanover Square. A history of the gardens and the surrounding area can be read on the board to the left as you enter. What it doesn't mention is that during the Cold War this peaceful oasis was a favoured haunt of KGB 'illegals', intelligence officers who operated in London under assumed names. Whenever they had information for their KGB masters they would leave a chalk mark on the rear horizontal slat of a particular bench, reputedly the second one to the right.

6 Have a quick, though discreet, glance at the bench, then keep ahead through the gardens. A few gravestones from the former burial ground are still scattered about the lawns.

As you arrive at the far side of the gardens, a visit to the stunningly ornate Church of the Immaculate Conception to the right is a must.
www.farmstreet.org.uk

7 Exit the gardens into Mount Street. Follow it right and keep ahead to turn right into Berkeley Square. Cross Hill Street and two doors along on the right is No. 44 Berkeley Square, The Clermont Club.

This house has been called 'the finest terrace house of London' and the brief glimpses you see through its windows confirm this sentiment. It was built in 1742 and designed by William Kent for Lady Isabella Finch, a maid of honour to Princess Amelia, George II's sister. The ghost of her head of household, resplendent in smart green uniform and handsome periwig, is said to wander the building just to ensure that things are running smoothly. Once he is satisfied that all is well, he simply melts away. The house is now an exclusive gaming club.

THE CLERMONT CLUB;

www.theclermontclub.com

8 Keep ahead through Berkeley Square and pause outside No. 50, now the premises of Maggs Bros Antiquarian Booksellers.

In Victorian times this sturdy-looking building had the dubious reputation of being the most haunted house in London. Many tales were told of the dreadful consequences that resulted from an encounter with its ghosts. A nobleman who scoffed at such tales vowed to spend a night alone in the haunted room. He had managed only a few hours when, a little after midnight, something appeared to him and scared him out of his wits. He was never able to say what that something was because his ordeal left him without the power of speech and such was his state of shock that he died shortly afterwards. Two sailors on shore leave broke into the house, which was then empty, and lay down to sleep in the haunted room. They were woken in the dead of night by determined footsteps stomping up the stairs. Suddenly the door burst open and a shapeless black mass oozed into the room. One of the sailors escaped but the other was later found impaled on the railings outside. He had leapt to his death rather than face the dreadful entity within. Today hideous supernatural beings appear to be a thing of the past, although a ghostly girl in a plaid dress has been known to skip down the stairs.

9 Proceed anti-clockwise around Berkeley Square. You can make a detour across to the garden at its centre where a board gives a detailed history. Otherwise, go right along Berkeley Street. At its end turn right on to Piccadilly and keep going till you arrive at Green Park Underground Station, where this walk finishes.

Wandering in Westminster

Westminster, the seat of British Government, is known for the Houses of Parliament, Westminster Abbey and the PM's home at 10 Downing Street.

This eventful walk encompasses two distinctive and contrasting aspects of Westminster. You will explore both the busy, well-known and well-trodden tourist sites but also venture into a more secretive world of quaint old streets, elegant houses and tucked-away squares. It begins by skirting the Houses of Parliament, then moves through a network of streets that take you back to a bygone age, contrasting strongly with the pomp and ceremony that is Parliament. These streets bring you to Westminster Abbey where, if you haven't done so, you should acquaint yourself with the famous figures that lie buried inside. Following a visit to the Cabinet War Rooms from where Winston Churchill directed World War II, you take a walk behind 10 Downing Street to learn of its ghosts, before coming to part of Whitehall Palace – where in 1649 the course of English history was changed when Charles I was beheaded outside.

I Leave Westminster Station via exit 4.

Look over the road at the clock tower of the Houses of Parliament, popularly known as Big Ben. In fact Big Ben itself is the 13-ton bell that hangs inside the tower – a reference to either Sir Benjamin Hall, the Commissioner of Works when the bell was hung in 1859, or to Ben Caunt, a prize-fighter who was particularly popular at the time.

2 Turn right on to Bridge Street, go over Canon Row and veer left over the traffic lights to keep ahead into Parliament Square.

To your left is the Palace of Westminster, better known as the Houses of Parliament. This fantasy of Gothic revival stands on the site of a royal palace that was the principal residence of the kings of England from the middle of the 11th century until 1512. The palace was destroyed by fire in 1834 and the present building rose from its ashes over the next 30 years. It is an intricate warren of nearly 1,200 rooms, 100 staircases and well over 2 miles (3.2km) of interlinking passages and corridors.

HOUSES OF PARLIAMENT;
SEE WEBSITE FOR DETAILS www.parliament.uk

3 Keep ahead into St Margaret's Street and pause alongside the statue of Oliver Cromwell.

The statue caused a bit of controversy when it was first mooted by Liberal Prime Minister Lord Roseberry in the

WHERE TO EAT

|O| THE RED LION,
48 Parliament Street;
Tel: 020 7930 5826.
A favoured haunt of civil servants, journalists, the occasional MP, and sundry tourists.

|O| WALKERS OF WHITEHALL,
15 Craig's Court;
Tel: 020 7925 0090.
www.walkersofwhitehall.co.uk
This air-conditioned bar doesn't tend to get as busy as the pubs on Whitehall. Traditional pub fare such as steaks and fish and chips, plus Mediterranean and Asian dishes.

1890s to mark the 300th anniversary of Cromwell's birth. Irish MPs objected because of Cromwell's ruthless reputation during his conquest of Ireland. Many English MPs agreed, on the grounds that Cromwell had orchestrated the trial and execution of Charles I. In the end Roseberry funded the statue himself. Cromwell holds a sword and a Bible, and his head is bowed in thought. It has been suggested that he is avoiding the accusatory gaze of Charles I, whose bust looks over at him from St Margaret's church opposite. Behind Cromwell is Westminster Hall, one of only two parts of the old palace to survive the 1834 fire. The walls date from 1097-99, when the building of the hall was ordered by William Rufus, son and successor of William the Conqueror.

DISTANCE **3 miles (4.8km)**

ALLOW **2 hours**

START **Westminster Underground Station**

FINISH **Westminster Underground Station**

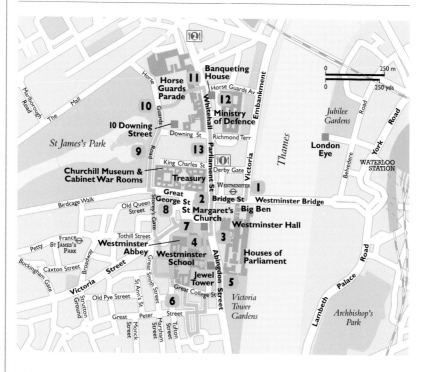

4 Backtrack and cross over the pedestrian crossing by the lamp post. Veer left on the other side and pass St Margaret's Church. Keep ahead past Westminster Abbey into Old Palace Yard. It was here on 31 January 1606 that Guy Fawkes, now the most famous of the Gunpowder Plot conspirators, was executed by being hanged, drawn and quartered. Continue forward and go down the steps to the left of the white building to enter the Jewel Tower.

Built for Edward III in 1365, this hidden away three-storey tower was designed to hold the king's private treasures and house his wardrobe. It is still one of the gems of Westminster and boasts an exquisite 14th-century ribbed vault which more than rewards a visit. The remains of the protective moat together with a medieval quay are still visible outside the building.

JEWEL TOWER;

www.english-heritage.org.uk/london

5 Backtrack, go up the steps, veer sharp right and walk past the railing on to the paved walkway. Go right into Great College Street, first left into Little College Street and right into Great Peter Street. Take the first left into Lord North Street.

On the wall between No.s 7 and 8, there is an air raid shelter sign from World War II. At the end of the street, on the right, is a green plaque to W T Stead, who lived here from 1904 to 1912. He was the father of modern tabloid journalism and a fearless campaigner for social change in late 19th-century Britain. He was also a committed spiritualist who may have predicted the future, and his own death, in two works of fiction. *How the Mail Steamer went Down in Mid Atlantic,* written in 1886, carried a footnote which lectured readers, "This is exactly what might take place and what will take place if the liners are sent to sea short of boats." Another tale, *From the Old World to the New,* written in 1892, told the story of a ship called the *Majestic* colliding with an iceberg. Much has been made of these two seemingly prophetic stories, as Stead himself was lost on board the *Titanic.*

6 Turn right into Smith Square, right on to Gayfere Street, and right again along Great Peter Street. Take the next turning left into Cowley Street, follow it as it bears left, turn right along Barton Street, then left into Great College Street. As it bears left, go right through the gate and walk anti-clockwise around College Green.

Around you are the buildings of Westminster School, dating from 1179 when the Benedictine monks of Westminster Abbey were required by Pope Alexander III to provide a small charity school. Former pupils include Ben Jonson (1573-1637), Sir Christopher Wren (1632-1723) and actor Sir John Gielgud (1904-2000).

7 Exit via the gates in the opposite left corner and turn right towards the Westminster Abbey Shop.

You might like to break now and visit the Abbey itself, established in 1065 by Edward the Confessor. The present building was begun by Henry III in the 13th century and was added to and extended over the next three centuries. All but two English monarchs since William the Conqueror were crowned here, and many are buried here, along with a host of other famous people.

WESTMINSTER ABBEY;

www.westminster-abbey.org

8 Keep ahead and go right on to Broad Sanctuary. Keep ahead to the traffic lights and cross the pedestrian crossing, off which bear left over Little George Street and go first right into Little Sanctuary.

A little way along on the right a stone gateway is all that remains of the 17th-century Westminster House of Correction or Bridewell, later known as Tothill Fields Prison. The prison features in William Hogarth's *Rake's Progress.*

9 Backtrack and bear right past the Queen Elizabeth II Conference Centre. Go right to Storey's Gate. Keep ahead over Great George Street, veer left and go right on to Horse Guards Road. On the right are The Cabinet War Rooms and Churchill Museum.

It was from these underground rooms that Winston Churchill and Britain's top politicians directed World War II. It is a place of echoing corridors where time, literally, stands still – all the clocks are frozen at 4:58, the time Cabinet was first held here on 15 October 1940. Many people experience sudden drops in temperature here, phantom footsteps have been heard, and imprints of military-style boots have appeared on freshly waxed floors. All in all, a spooky place to dally.

CHURCHILL MUSEUM;
DAILY 9.30-5 www.cwr.iwm.org.uk

10 Exit the War Rooms, turn right then bear right on to the gravel of Horse Guards Parade.

The red-brick building to the right behind the trees is the back of 10 Downing Street, the residence of the Prime Minister. In 1732 George II gave 10 Downing Street to his Prime Minister, First Lord of the Treasury, Sir Robert Walpole (1676-1745). Over the years the house has been extended and altered.

11 Keep ahead through Horse Guards Arch, a history of which can be read on the white wall boards to the left and right on the other side.

There have been recent rumours of ghostly goings-on in the Horse Guards stables. Bridles hanging on the wall have been known to start to swing in unison. In July 2007 the Household Cavalry Museum opened here to provide visitors with a 'behind-the-scenes' look at the ceremonial and operational role of the Household Cavalry Regiment.

CHURCHILL MUSEUM;
www.householdcavalrymuseum.org.uk

12 Pass out through the gates, turn left along Whitehall, go over the crossing, bear right, cross Horse Guards Avenue and go left through the gates of the Banqueting House.

This is the only visible section of Whitehall Palace to have survived a devastating fire in 1698. The Banqueting House was built by Inigo Jones in 1622, and 13 years later Charles I commissioned the artist Peter Paul Rubens to paint the ceiling, to glorify aspects of the king's reign. The ceiling is, without a doubt, the building's crowning glory. Ironically, it was through a window of the Banqueting House on 30 January 1649 that King Charles stepped out on to a specially constructed scaffold and was publically beheaded.

BANQUETING HOUSE; MON-SAT 10-7
www.hrp.org.uk/banquetinghouse

13 Leave the Banqueting House, turn left on to Whitehall and keep ahead along Parliament Street until you arrive at Westminster Underground Station, where this walk ends.

A Brush with Royalty

St James's is London's royal village. It has palaces, grand homes, exclusive shops and some delightful secret passages. In short, it is full of surprises.

The walk begins on what is widely considered to be one of London's most exquisite streets, Queen Anne's Gate. Having learnt how a case of mistaken identity led to a statue in the street being abused by local vagabonds, you stroll through St James's Park to admire the exotic waterfowl while keeping your eyes peeled for the headless spectre that has been known to rise from its lake. Your next destination will be St James's Palace, before twisting and turning through a warren of backstreets to arrive at the scene of a notorious 17th-century murder. Having made the acquaintance of the Grand Old Duke of York, you will move on to admire the statue of Charles I and discover something of its bizarre history, before pausing for refreshment while enjoying a peek into the private life of Sherlock Holmes. As a whole, this walk of delightful contrasts will introduce you to a hidden side of a fairly well-known part of London, so be sure that you take the time to savour and absorb its unique ambience.

1 Cross Petty France by the pedestrian crossing, keep ahead into Queen Anne's Gate and follow it as it bears right. This delightful street with its elegant houses, many of which have ornate wooden door canopies, dates from the early 18th century. Note the faces displaying all manner of odd expressions that look down at you from the first floor of each building. Pause half way down on the right by the statue of Queen Anne.

Erected in 1705 and moved to its current position in 1810, this statue once suffered an appalling case of mistaken identity. Local street urchins came to believe that it was in fact Queen 'Bloody' Mary, and they took revenge for her persecutions of Protestants by frequently pelting the statue with stones. She soon lost her nose and right arm. In 1861 the Office of Works commissioned a restoration and had her name, ANNA REGINA, carved on the plinth to clear up the confusion. It meant little to the local children, however, and the stone-throwing continued for at least another generation. There is a local tradition that on the night of 1 August, the anniversary of Anne's death, the statue steps from the pedestal and marches up and down the street three times.

2 Follow the street as it bears left, go down Cockpit Steps and turn left on to Birdcage Walk. Be sure to keep an eye open for the headless female phantom that has been known to drift along here. Go over the traffic lights and ahead into St James's Park, a full history

of which can be read on the board to the right. Walk on to the bridge and pause over the lake, which dates from 1827, when the park was landscaped by John Nash.

The headless woman who haunts Cockpit Steps is also said to frequent the lake. She rises from the water, glides across the surface and, as she reaches the bank, begins to run towards the bushes, where she vanishes. Tradition holds that she is the ghost of the wife of a sergeant at the nearby barracks who murdered her in the 1780s. Having cut off her head, he buried it at a secret location and then threw her body into the lake.

3 Continue over the bridge and keep ahead, leaving St James's Park, and cross over The Mall. Buckingham Palace is to your left and makes a worthwhile detour. Otherwise, keep ahead along Marlborough Road and go left into

DISTANCE 2.75 miles (4.4km)

ALLOW 2 hours

START St James's Park Underground Station, Broadway and Park Exit

FINISH Embankment Underground Station

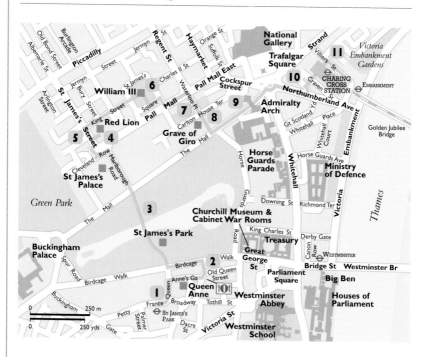

Cleveland Row to pause outside the gatehouse of St James's Palace.

To the right of the gatehouse you can see the stained glass of the windows of the Chapel Royal. It was here in September 1997 that Princess Diana's coffin lay in state, prior to her funeral at Westminster Abbey. Thousands of grief-stricken people filed into the palace to sign the books of condolence. Several came out visibly shaken, claiming that they had seen Princess Diana's face staring from

the top right corner of an oil portrait of Charles I. Whether or not this sighting was caused by a trick of the light combined with the high emotions of that week, no one could say. But several witnesses claimed that when they had tried to get a closer look, the face of the princess had suddenly vanished.

BUCKINGHAM PALACE;

LIMITED SUMMER OPENING

www.royal.gov.uk

ST JAMES'S PALACE;

NOT OPEN TO PUBLIC

WHERE TO EAT

🍽 THE CROWN AND TWO CHAIRMEN,
39 Dartmouth Street;
Tel: 020 7222 8694.
The decor in this pub shows signs of wear and might be a little dated, but it makes for a nice break before heading off in search of the ghosts of St James's Park. The food is basic pub fare – not exceptional but filling.

4 Walk away from the palace gatehouse and bear right over St James's Street via the two crossings. Go past Berry Brothers and Rudd Ltd, after which turn right into Pickering Place.

The star on the wall plaque on the right as you enter commemorates the Texan Republic's Legation which was based here until Texas joined the Union in 1845. This secluded courtyard dates back to the 1830s.

5 Exit Pickering Place and go right. Keep ahead and go right into King Street. On arrival in St James's Square cautiously cross to the garden at its centre and pause to look up at the statue of William III (1650-1701).

What is intriguing about this statue is that it depicts William's final moments frozen for evermore – or at least for as long as the statue stands. The king died of injuries sustained in Richmond Park when his horse stumbled on a molehill.

The statue shows the horse's head skewing right, freezing the first moments of the king's fall. The molehill over which it tripped can be seen behind the horse's rear leg.

6 Veer right at the statue to exit the gardens, a full history of which can be read on the board by the gate. Cross the road and bear left, then right and left again on to Pall Mall. Go over the crossing and pause at the junction with Waterloo Place.

It was on this corner on the night of 12 February 1681 that Thomas Thynne of Longleat was shot as he passed along Pall Mall in his coach. His assassins were three hired hands in the employ of Count Köningsmark, who was envious of Thynne's forthcoming marriage to wealthy heiress Lady Elizabeth Ogle. The count hoped that, with his rival out of the way, he might marry her himself. All four men were apprehended a week later, but at the subsequent trial Köningsmark bribed the jury and was acquitted. The other three were hanged at the site of their crime.

7 Keep ahead through Waterloo Place and pause by the railings to the left of the large cream building.

In front of the tree is the tombstone erected by German ambassador, Leopold von Hoesch, in 1934 to mark the burial place of his beloved dog, Ciro. Two years later von Hoesch died from a stroke, brought on by strained Anglo-German relations and his new Nazi masters. As the only surviving Nazi monument in London it was used in World War II by an American reporter to illustrate the British temperament. As he explained, the British might hate the Nazis but desecrating the grave of a dog just wasn't on.

8 Go down the steps to the left and look up to admire the Duke of York's Column.

The statue atop the column depicts Frederic, Duke of York, the second son of George III and Commander-in-Chief of the British Army. However, he is probably best remembered as the Grand Old Duke of York from the popular nursery rhyme.

9 Keep ahead and cross The Mall by the traffic lights. Bear left and keep ahead over Horse Guards to pass through Admiralty Arch. On arrival at Whitehall go over the crossing and bear left over the next lights to pause alongside the statue of Charles I.

The statue was made in 1633 by the sculptor Hubert Le Sueur. When Charles was beheaded in 1649 the statue was sold to a scrap-metal merchant, John Rivett, who did a roaring trade in artefacts such as knife handles and candlesticks that he claimed were made from its melted metal. But with the restoration of the monarchy under Charles II he presented the statue undamaged to the new king and was rewarded by being made the King's Brazier. Charles had the statue re-erected on its current site in 1675. A plaque

behind the statue marks the spot from which distances to London are marked.

10 Bear right at the statue, go over the crossing, turn right over the next crossing and keep ahead into Northumberland Avenue. Go left over Northumberland Street to arrive at the Sherlock Holmes pub.

In the upstairs room is a replica of the sitting room at 221b Baker Street. Look at the Holmes memorabilia on the walls.

11 Leave the pub and go left along Craven Passage, over Craven Street. Pass through The Arches and turn right down Villiers Street to arrive at Embankment Station, where this walk ends.

Ghosts and Greasepaint

In London's Theatreland it can seem as though the whole world is jostling for space. Yet, down a hidden alleyway or courtyard, old London still exists.

This walk begins at the bustling hub of the West End, Piccadilly Circus, and goes immediately to the restaurant where Dr Watson first heard of Sherlock Holmes. From here it snakes its way past the elegant frontage of one of London's most beautiful theatres, before taking you across Trafalgar Square and into some of the most intriguing alleyways in London. These include a genuine throwback to the 17th century that many people pass on a daily basis and don't even realize is there. Tales of ghosts and murder crop up regularly, while the opportunity to visit the churches of St Martin-in-the-Fields and St Paul's Covent Garden should not be passed up. All in all, an eventful stroll that will introduce you to the more hidden places of one of London's best-known neighbourhoods. The bustle of modern London will be a constant companion, but a sudden turn into a secret courtyard will provide a portal to a bygone age.

1 Leave Piccadilly station and stand by the statue of Eros. From there, cross over to peek inside the door of the Criterion Brasserie.

Designed by Thomas Verity in the 1870s, the opulent mirrored and marble interior with golden ceiling is truly stunning. It was here in Arthur Conan Doyle's *A Study in Scarlet* that Dr Watson met with young Stamford, an encounter that led to his being introduced to an eccentric character by the name of Sherlock Holmes who was looking for someone to share rooms with.

2 Go left in front of the Criterion and turn right into Haymarket. Cross to its left side and keep ahead over Panton and Orange streets. Pause on arrival at the portico of Theatre Royal Haymarket.

This beautiful building dates from 1821 and was designed by royal architect John Nash. It saw some of its greatest successes between 1853 and 1878 under the management of John Baldwin Buckstone, who was a great friend of Charles Dickens and whose ghost is said to wander the theatre. He has been seen watching performances from the royal box; his disembodied voice has been heard rehearsing in his old dressing room; and his phantom form has appeared in the auditorium where he keeps a watchful eye on the comings and goings at the theatre that he evidently still considers to be *his*.

THEATRE ROYAL;

www.trh.co.uk

3 Go next left into Suffolk Place, which was rebuilt by John Nash in the 1820s. Follow it as it turns left and continue to the top right building, No. 15, where there is a plaque on the wall to the artist Richard Dadd (1817-1886).

Richard's father, Robert, brought his family to live here in 1834. Eight years later Richard undertook a tour of Europe and the Middle East, in the course of which he began to experience paranoid delusions. He became convinced that divine forces were urging him to do battle with the devil, who could assume any form he desired. On his return to England Richard Dadd's concerned father took him on what he hoped would prove a recuperative break to Cobham in Kent. Little did he realize that his son now believed him to be the devil. At 11pm on 28 August 1843, as the two men walked in the countryside, Richard Dadd stabbed his father to death. Apprehended, he was declared insane and spent the rest of his life in Broadmoor Asylum.

DISTANCE **2.25 miles (3.6km)**

ALLOW **I hour 45 minutes**

START **Piccadilly Underground Station**

FINISH **Charing Cross Station**

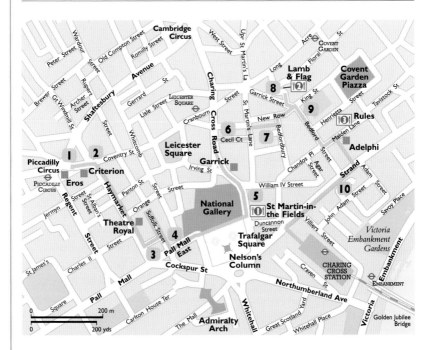

4 Backtrack and continue walking to the end of Suffolk Place. Go left into Pall Mall East and keep ahead into Trafalgar Square.

The square is dominated by the column to Admiral Horatio Lord Nelson, whose death in the closing moments of his greatest victory at the Battle of Trafalgar in 1805 the square commemorates. On the left through the square, after the National Gallery, is the church of St Martin-in-the-Fields, on St Martin's

Place. It dates from 1724 and is worth a detour to visit.

ST MARTIN-IN-THE-FIELDS;

www.stmartin-in-the-fields.org

5 Cross St Martin's Place via the traffic lights outside the National Portrait Gallery, bear left and pass to the left of the memorial to Edith Cavell. Continue ahead over William IV Street into Charing Cross Road. You'll reach the Garrick Theatre, built in 1889 for W S Gilbert (of Gilbert & Sullivan fame).

The theatre is haunted by former manager Arthur Bourchier (1864-1927), whose ghost has been known to give actors a good-luck pat on the shoulder before they go on stage. During a 1990s refurbishment, a group of builders working on the upper floors were startled when Bourchier appeared before them, fixed them with a stern stare and then swiftly vanished.

6 Continue along Charing Cross Road and go next right into Cecil Court. This picturesque late Victorian thoroughfare is a book lover's paradise lined with antiquarian bookshops. Watkin's Books at No. 19 claims to be the oldest occultist and mystical bookshop in the world.

At No. 23 at midday on Friday 3 March 1961, the body of part-time shop assistant Mrs Elsie May Batten was found in the curtained-off rear of the antique shop. An 18-inch (45cm) antique dagger was protruding from her chest. The shop's owner, Louis Meier, remembered a young man who had shown an interest in a particular dress sword and some daggers in his shop the previous day. The sword was now missing. It turned up in a gun shop on the opposite side of the court, where the son of the owner told police that a man had brought it into his shop that morning. Using these witness descriptions, the police compiled England's first Identikit picture and released it to the media. On 8 March 1961 PC Cole, who was on duty in Old Compton Street, recognized 21-year-old Edwin Bush as being the face on the picture and arrested him. Bush was subsequently hanged for committing Elsie Batten's murder.

7 Go through Cecil Court and turn left along St Martin's Lane. Cross to its right side and two doors past the Green Man and French Horn, go right into Goodwin's Court.

This bucolic place, with its bow-fronted houses, most dating from the 17th century, really is a throwback to a bygone age. Gaslit Goodwin's Court is particularly atmospheric by night.

8 Go left along Bedfordbury, right into New Row and left on to Garrick Street. Take the first right into Rose Street. Directly ahead of you is the Lamb and Flag pub.

This true gem of old London used to be known as the Bucket of Blood – bare-

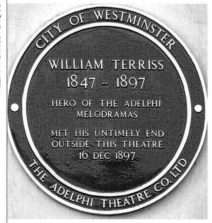

CITY OF WESTMINSTER

WILLIAM TERRISS
1847 – 1897

HERO OF THE ADELPHI
MELODRAMAS

MET HIS UNTIMELY END
OUTSIDE THIS THEATRE
16 DEC 1897

THE ADELPHI THEATRE CO. LTD

knuckle fights were once held here. In 1679 the poet John Dryden was almost beaten to death in narrow Lazenby Court to the right of the pub by a group of thugs hired by the Earl of Rochester, in revenge for a satirical verse he believed Dryden had written about him. You can read a history of the pub and the attack on a slanted board on the roof of the passageway – although you may find yourself in the way of pedestrians whose progress you are blocking.

9 Backtrack to Garrick Street, turn left and keep ahead into Bedford Street, passing on the left the gates to St Paul's Church, Covent Garden. Keep ahead over Henrietta Street and go next left into Maiden Lane. A little past Exchange Court, go past the stage door of the Adelphi Theatre.

The green wall plaque commemorates William Terriss, one of the most celebrated actors of the late Victorian era. On 16 December 1897 Terriss arrived for his evening performance in the play *Secret Service* at the theatre and was unlocking the door to the right of the plaque when Richard Prince, a bit-part actor who had developed a pathological envy of Terriss's success, stepped from the shadows and stabbed him twice in the back. The wounds were superficial, but as Terriss turned to confront his attacker Prince lunged again and this time pierced his heart. Onlookers, who had mistaken the first two stabs as pats on the back, now realized what was happening and rushed forward to restrain Prince. But

Terris was beyond help and died shortly afterwards in the arms of his leading lady, Jessie Milward. On hearing of his death, the actress Ellen Terry later commented, "Poor dear Terriss – I do hope he lived long enough to realize he had been murdered. How he would have enjoyed it!" Terriss's ghost roams Maiden Lane, and the Adelphi Theatre.

10 Backtrack to Exchange Court, pass through it and turn right on to Strand. Cross to its opposite side and keep ahead to Charing Cross Station and the walk's end.

Museums and the Macabre

Much of this walk is spent indoors, making it a good tour to save for rainy days when you might not want to spend time out on the streets.

Aim to do this walk from Tuesday to Friday, when all the museums are open. It begins with a visit to a macabre museum where you will find yourself staring at pieces of pickled people preserved in jars and cabinets, as well as viewing the skeleton of one of the capital's most notorious 18th-century villains. Having sated your appetite for the ghoulish, you can embroil yourself in one of the most eclectic collections of art treasures and architectural curiosities ever assembled under one London roof, put together by Sir John Soane in the house he bought in 1812. From here you wander through busy streets and a tucked-away square to hear a chilling tale of a suicide that might have been murder. Having gazed at a soaring building that inspired George Orwell, you step back into the distant past at one of the largest collections of Egyptian artefacts in the world. The grand finale of this unusual walk is the opportunity to gaze at the auto-icon of Jeremy Bentham, sitting inside a sturdy wooden display case, and wearing his best 18th-century clothes. What's an auto-icon? Read on.

1 Exit the station and go left along Kingsway. Turn left at the traffic lights, go along Remnant Street, then turn right into Lincoln's Inn Fields and pause outside No.s 59 and 60, Lindsey House.

Lindsey House was built in 1641 as one large property but divided into two houses in 1752, a renovation reflected in the dividing wall that runs down the middle of the central windows. Spencer Perceval, the only English Prime Minister to have been assassinated, lived here prior to taking office in 1809. There is a difficult-to-discern brown plaque to him on the wall of No. 60.

2 Continue ahead and cross over Sardinia Street into Portsmouth Street where a little way along on the left is the Old Curiosity Shop.

Built in 1567 as two cottages on the lands of the Duchess of Portsmouth, this is certainly one of London's most venerable buildings but the claim emblazoned on its front that it was immortalized by Charles Dickens in his book *The Old Curiosity Shop* is somewhat misleading. The shop Dickens wrote of was located near Leicester Square and was, according to Dickens at the end of the book, 'long ago pulled down'.

3 Backtrack into Lincoln's Inn Fields, go right and a little way along turn right again to enter the Royal College of Surgeons. Check in at the desk and walk up to the first floor to visit the Hunterian Museum, England's largest

WHERE TO EAT

🍴 **SHIP TAVERN,**
12 Gate Street;
Tel: 020 7405 1992.
Hidden away in a narrow alleyway just a short walk from Holborn Station, this cosy hostelry is very much a traditional London pub, one of the few to have survived the recent advent of theme bars and gastropubs.

🍴 **THE FRIEND AT HAND,**
2-4 Herbrand Street;
Tel: 020 7837 5524.
Another hidden pub that features on the walk – stop here to contemplate its history and look for the ghost. The food on offer is pleasant pub grub, filling as opposed to fancy.

and most important collection of both human and zoological anatomical and pathological specimens.

The exhibits, although fascinating, are most certainly not for the squeamish. Among them is the skeleton of Jonathan Wilde (1689-1725), the self-styled thief-taker general of London who, while pretending to be Britain's most successful capturer of criminals, was in fact a receiver of stolen goods, which he would then sell back to their owners. He even informed on those who had stolen on his behalf. He was finally brought to justice in February 1725 and a huge crowd turned out to watch his execution on

DISTANCE 3 miles (4.8km)

ALLOW 2 hours

START Holborn Underground Station, Kingsway Exit

FINISH Euston Square Underground Station

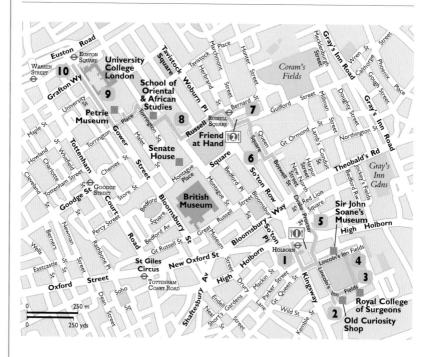

24 May that year. His body was sold to the surgeons for dissection.

ROYAL COLLEGE OF SURGEONS;

TUE-SAT 10-5 www.rcseng.ac.uk/museums

4 Exit the Royal College of Surgeons. Go over the road and through the gates to cross to the covered porch at the centre of the gardens of Lincoln's Inn Fields. In the reign of Elizabeth I executions were carried out here, and the ghostly screams of those who died are said to echo across this spot at night.

Keep ahead through the gates, go over the road and veer left to the Sir John Soane Museum.

Soane, the architect of the Bank of England, reconstructed this house in 1792 and amassed a veritable treasure trove of beautiful, curious and instructive artefacts. These included originals of William Hogarth's *The Rake's Progress* and *Election Campaign*. He left instructions that, upon his death, the house and its contents were to be preserved as a public

museum, and to step through the doors is to be transported back to London in the early 19th century.

SIR JOHN SOANE MUSEUM;
TUE-SAT 10-5 www.soane.org

5 Leave the museum and turn right. Go right again on to Gate Street. You can read a history of the area on the outer wall of the Ship Tavern which you pass. Go through Little Turnstile to the right of the pub, bear left to cross High Holborn via the traffic lights and keep ahead along Procter Street. Keep ahead into Drake Street and go left then right over the two crossings to walk the full length of Boswell Street. Bear left into Queen Square and pause on the corner by the Queen's Larder.

This tavern is so named because Queen Charlotte, consort of George III, rented cellar space beneath the building to store some of her husband's favourite foods while he was being treated nearby at his physician Dr Willis's house during his bouts of insanity. You can read its history on the board outside.

6 Continue clockwise round the square and exit via the passage to the left of No. 23. Go left on to Guildford Street and first right into Herbrand Street. A little way along on the right is the Friend at Hand, a pub formerly known as the Globe, which was built in 1735.

In 1836 the publican, William Thornton, being ill in bed from over-consumption,

sent his barmaid to the cellar to fetch liquor. When she returned she found him dead with his throat cut. The coroner accepted a verdict of suicide, although the fact that William's ghost still walks the pub suggests there may have been more to his final moments than the maid was willing to admit. A full history of the pub and of famous figures who have drunk here can be read on the board outside.

7 Continue along Herbrand Street, go left on to Bernard Street and cross the traffic lights into Russell Square towards the public toilet. Walk past it and, on arrival at the second set of lights, be sure to make a detour through the gate into the gardens to read the history of the square and surroundings on the information board. Go over the lights, bear left and first right through the gates to look up at the soaring white exterior of Senate House.

Senate House was designed by Charles Holden in 1937 and known locally as the 'Big House in Bloomsbury'. Although it now houses the administrative buildings of University College London, during World War II it was occupied by the Ministry of Information – to which journalists came for news about the war. Among those who visited was George Orwell who used it as the model for the Ministry of Truth in his book *1984*.

8 Backtrack left through the gates and keep ahead into Thornhaugh Street. Pass the School of Oriental and African Studies building and go left into Woburn

Square, where you can read its history on a board in the gardens. Go over the ramp and turn right into Torrington Square. Turn left on to Byng Place and take the first right into Malet Place. Towards its top on the left you will find the Petrie Museum.

The museum is home to the greatest collection of Egyptian and Sudanese archaeological artefacts in the world and displays some 80,000 exhibits. It illustrates life in the Nile Valley from prehistory through the time of the pharaohs, the Ptolemaic, Roman and Coptic periods to the Islamic period.

PETRIE MUSEUM;

TUE-FRI 1-5, SAT 10-1 www.petrie.ucl.ac.uk

9 Backtrack along Malet Place, go right on to Torrington Place and first right along Gower Street. Keep going until you arrive at the main gates of University College London.

The impressive Wilkins Building ahead of you dates from 1825. Pass to its right and go in through the door marked Wilkins Building South Cloisters. Turn right then left and pause before one of London's most curious relics, a glass-fronted wooden case that contains the skeleton – or auto-icon as he called it in his will – of Jeremy Bentham, one of the founders of University College. He is dressed in his usual clothes and holds a stick. Although the face is made of wax, his mummified head still exists and is locked away in the college safe. His full story, and the tale of how he instructed his remains to be preserved in this bizarre exhibitionist manner after his death, can be read on the exhibition boards that surround him.

10 Backtrack to the entrance on Gower Street, turn right through the gates and keep going until you arrive at Euston Square Underground Station.

Curses in Covent Garden

Covent Garden is one of London's most vibrant neighbourhoods. This walk uncovers some of the lore and legends associated with the area.

Covent Garden is home to some of the capital's most beautiful theatre buildings. On this walk you'll pause for a moment outside London's oldest working theatre and investigate its resident ghost, perhaps the most famous theatre ghost in London. The walk also takes in a former burial ground that is now a pleasant garden and children's play area. Having passed the place where Bram Stoker was working when he wrote the chilling tale of *Dracula*, we descend into the twilight world of the basement levels of Somerset House, before paying a visit to a hidden antiquity of uncertain age. The penultimate destination is the Egyptian obelisk, Cleopatra's Needle, London's oldest monument, where you can search for the shadowy figure that is said to haunt it. Although not directly on the route, it is well worth making a slight detour to enjoy the vibrancy of the Covent Garden Market Piazza. Here you can visit some intriguing shops and enjoy the antics of street performers ranging from jugglers to human statues.

1 Exit Holborn Underground Station and go left along Kingsway. Go right at the traffic lights and keep straight into Great Queen Street. Cross to its left side and go left on to Drury Lane.

On 7 June 1665, Samuel Pepys walked along Drury Lane and saw 'two or three houses marked with a red cross upon the doors and "Lord have mercy upon us" writ there'. The cross meant that the plague had struck the household. By the end of that year the Great Plague, as it became known, had claimed the lives of more than 90,000 Londoners.

2 Continue along Drury Lane, cross via the zebra crossing and proceed into Drury Lane Gardens.

Once the burial ground for St Martin-in-the-Fields, it had become terribly overcrowded by the 19th century. In the 1850s London's overflowing and unsightly burial grounds were closed to further interments and 30 years later many of them, including this one, were converted to public gardens. Today a children's playground occupies the site and only the two buildings on either side of the gates – one a former mortuary and one a former keeper's lodge – remember its more macabre past.

3 Leave the gardens and go right along Drury Lane. Take the next right into Russell Street. Cross to its left side, turn left on to Catherine Street and pause in the portico of the Theatre Royal, Drury Lane.

WHERE TO EAT

🍽 SARASTRO,
126 Drury Lane;
Tel: 020 7836 0101.
www.sarastro-restaurant.com
Flamboyant restaurant with gold fabric draped from the ceiling. Dine in one of 14 opera boxes.

🍽 RIVER TERRACE CAFÉ,
Somerset House, Strand;
Tel: 020 7845 4600.
www.somersethouse.org.uk
Enjoy magnificent views across the Thames at this alfresco café.

Founded in 1663, this is the oldest working theatre in London, although the present building dates from 1812. Its ghosts include that of Joseph Grimaldi (1778-1837), the father of modern clownery, who has been known to administer a playful kick to actors, cleaners and usherettes. Another is that of Dan Leno (1861-1904), who suffered from chronic incontinence, which he disguised with copious amounts of lavender water. He sometimes glides invisibly by performers leaving the smell of his perfume in his ghostly wake. But the theatre's most famous ghost is that of the Man in Grey, a limping, bewigged apparition who wears a grey riding coat and a tri-cornered hat. He frequently appears during daylight in the upper circle, which he crosses and then melts into the wall. His appearances are sought after since he presages a successful run.

OPPOSITE: COVENT GARDEN PIAZZA

DISTANCE **2.25 miles (3.6km)**

ALLOW **2 hours**

START **Holborn Underground Station, Kingsway Exit**

FINISH **Embankment Underground Station**

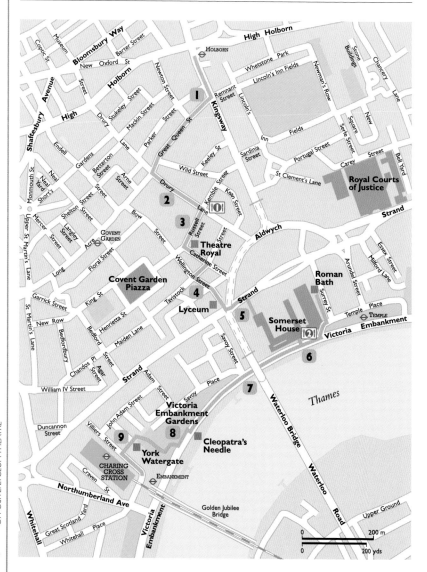

4 Go first right along Tavistock Street, then turn left into Wellington Street and cross over to its right side. Descend the hill and pause in the portico of the Lyceum Theatre.

In the 19th century Sir Henry Irving, the first actor to be knighted, frequently performed here. It was while working at the Lyceum as Irving's actor manager that Bram Stoker wrote *Dracula*.

5 Walk to the end of Wellington Street, turn left on to Strand and immediately cross it via the crossing. Bear left and keep ahead to turn right through the gates of Somerset House.

So-named because it stands on the site of a palace built between 1547 and 1550 by Edward Seymour, Protector Somerset, it was at this palace that Oliver Cromwell died on the night of 30 August 1658. As he breathed his last a colossal storm, the like of which had not been witnessed for hundreds of years, shook the capital. Rumour was rife that Cromwell had in fact been carried from this world on the wings of the storm. The present building dates from 1775 and was designed by Sir William Chambers. Parts of it were given over to use by various Admiralty offices and Lord Nelson (1758-1805) was a frequent visitor. He continues to pay the occasional visit on bright summer mornings when his ghost has sometimes been seen striding jauntily across the courtyard. Keep to the left of the fountains and enter the door in the far left corner to descend the Stamp Stair,

which once gave access to the Stamp Office. Here documents and newspapers were given the official stamp to ensure that the correct tax had been paid. A history of the office can be read on the wall to the left as you go through the door.

SOMERSET HOUSE;
OPEN DAILY 10-6 www.somersethouse.org.uk

6 Turn right off the stairs, right along the corridor and exit Somerset House left on to Victoria Embankment. Bear left into Temple Place and enter Strand Lane where on the right is the Roman Bath.

It is not known for certain how old this antiquity actually is, although it is generally referred to as Roman. People were certainly enjoying cold plunges in its waters in the 18th century and William Weddell, the renowned collector, even died from 'a sudden internal chill' while bathing here in April 1792. A full history can be read on the board on the railings and the bath can be viewed through the window.

7 Backtrack to Victoria Embankment and cross it via the pedestrian crossing. Bear right and keep ahead under Waterloo Bridge to arrive at Cleopatra's Needle.

This obelisk was originally erected in the Egyptian city of Heliopolis around 1460 BC by Thotmes III. The Romans moved it to the City of Alexandria in 12 BC but it was later toppled and lay prostrate on the sands for centuries. Fortuitously this preserved most of its hieroglyphics from the effects of weathering. In 1819 it was presented to the British people, although it wasn't until September 1877 that efforts were made to transport it to this country. But from the moment it left Egypt it seemed that some ancient curse had been loosed from the Needle. It was almost lost in a storm in the Bay of Biscay when six sailors, whose names are on the plinth of the Needle, died. It reached London in January 1878 and was erected on this spot. On 4 September 1917, bombs from the first German air raid on London fell nearby and the shrapnel damage is still clearly visible on the sphinx to the right of the Needle. Before you leave, be sure to cast a glance beyond for the ghostly figure that is said to race across the riverside terrace and throw itself over the parapet, although no splash is ever heard.

8 Cross busy Victoria Embankment via the zebra crossing directly by Cleopatra's Needle (undoubtedly one of the most frightening parts of this walk!). Bear left and go right into Victoria Embankment Gardens. You can read the story of how this land was reclaimed from the Thames in the 19th century on the boards to the right. Keep straight on, but pause by the York Watergate.

This was built in 1626 for George Villiers, 1st Duke of Buckingham, whose house stood beyond it. It once gave direct access from his garden to the Thames, the waters of which lapped around the gate until the 19th century. Turn and look at its distance from the river today and you begin to appreciate the feat of engineering achieved by the Victorians in constructing the Embankment.

9 Pass to the right of York Watergate. Go through the gate, left on to Watergate Walk and left down Villiers Street to arrive at Embankment Station, where this walk concludes.

69

Ghosts by Gaslight

It is possible to find tranquillity in the heart of London but menace lurks around the corner in the dark alleyways and creepy courtyards.

In the Middle and Inner Temples, close to the Thames, old buildings and dreamy courtyards are hidden away from the rush of modern London. In the 19th century, Charles Dickens wrote of the area 'who enters here leaves noise behind'. That description still holds true today, and to walk these lanes and passages is to follow in the footsteps of both famous and forgotten figures. A highlight of the walk is the wonderful Temple Church, which dates back to 1185 and recently became notorious throughout the world when it was featured in the book and subsequent film of Dan Brown's *The Da Vinci Code*. As well as history and ghostly tales, the walk also features two of London's most infamous characters. You will view the building where a leading contender for the mantle of Jack the Ripper once worked, and if that's not enough to send shivers down your spine, you will end your journey in one of London's most sinister little alleyways to see the spine-chilling site of Sweeney Todd's barber shop.

1 Turn left out of Temple station, go up the steps, turn right, cross the road and keep ahead along Temple Place.

The ornate building you come to on the left is the former Astor Estate Office which despite its Tudor appearance dates from 1895, when it was built for the immensely wealthy William Waldorf Astor. Note the gilded caravel weathervane representing the vessel that took Christopher Columbus to America.

2 Bear left and immediately right through the small gate to enter the Middle Temple, one of the Inns of Court. These ancient societies are where barristers – the wigged and robed practitioners of the art of advocacy in England's courts – have their chambers. Almost immediately, the roar of modern London is reduced to a distant murmur. Keep ahead and go left through a second gate, to ascend the steps and pass between the beautiful Temple Gardens on your right and Garden Court on your left. Go up the second flight of steps, veer right and pause outside the wonderfully ornate gates of Middle Temple Dining Hall.

This jewel of Tudor architecture was formally opened by Elizabeth I in 1576. On 2 February 1602 *Twelfth Night* by William Shakespeare is said to have premièred here, and there is a good chance that Shakespeare himself took part in the performance. During renovation work in the 19th century, workmen uncovered an old box hidden near the

WHERE TO EAT

[◎] **THE SEVEN STARS,**
53 Carey Street;
Tel: 020 7242 8521.
Slightly off your route, this tiny pub recently celebrated its 400th anniversary. It has bags of character and offers seasonal dishes that might include oysters or steak.

[◎] **YE OLD COCK TAVERN,**
22 Fleet Street;
Tel: 020 7333 8570.
A long and narrow Fleet Street pub.

[◎] **THE CITTIE OF YORKE,**
22 High Holborn;
Tel: 020 7242 7670.
A little way past Chancery Lane Station, this place is more like a baronial hall than a London pub.

rafters. When they opened it they found a human skeleton inside. How it came to be there is just one of the many mysteries a place this old is inevitably privy to.

3 Go left along Middle Temple Lane and first right into Pump Court – pumps for fighting Temple fires once stood here.

Unfortunately, on 26 January 1679 the entire court burnt down because the Thames was frozen and the fire pumps were unable to get sufficient water. The buildings around the court were rebuilt in 1686 and a fine sundial high up on the

OPPOSITE: CHOIR STALLS IN ST CLEMENT DANES CHURCH

DISTANCE **2.5 miles (4km)**

ALLOW **1 hour 45 minutes**

START **Temple Underground Station**

FINISH **Chancery Lane Underground Station**

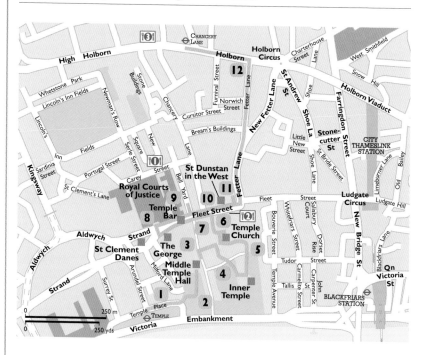

left wall is emblazoned with the timely reminder 'Shadows we are and Like shadows depart'.

4 On the opposite side of Pump Court, go right through the cloisters, which were reconstructed by Sir Christopher Wren following the fire of 1679. Go down the steps, turn left, left again and emerge into the large square where to your right you can see the Temple Gardens. You have now arrived in the Inner Temple. Bear

diagonally right over the road, pass Paper Buildings, and keep diagonally right to arrive at No. 9 King's Bench Walk.

These were once the chambers of 31-year-old barrister Montague John Druitt who committed suicide by drowning himself in the River Thames in November 1888. In 1894 Melville McNaughton, the Chief Constable of the Metropolitan Police, named Druitt as his favoured suspect for being Jack the Ripper, albeit the main reason for his

suspicions appears to have been Druitt's suicide coinciding with the last murder.

5 Backtrack to Paper Buildings and keep ahead to turn left through the arch and emerge into the wide-open pedestrian courtyard, where to your right is the Temple Church.

This round church was built in 1185 by the Knights Templar, the monastic military order after which the Temple area is named. Inside can be seen stone effigies of these Soldiers of Christ. Above the tomb of Edmund Plowden (16th-century lawyer and legal scholar), directly opposite the door through which you enter, a narrow slit in the wall was once the penitentiary cell where disobedient Templars were reputedly starved to death. The church and its surroundings were featured in Dan Brown's bestseller, *The Da Vinci Code*, and the church was used

as a location in the subsequent movie, starring Tom Hanks.

TEMPLE CHURCH;
SEE WEBSITE FOR OPENING TIMES
www.templechurch.com

6 Leave the church and walk clockwise around it to enter the churchyard.

Over by the railings is the tomb of 18th-century poet and playwright Oliver Goldsmith. A plaque at the foot of the tomb provides a little biographical detail about him. In the left corner immediately past Goldsmith Buildings is the back door of the Old Cock Tavern. In the 1980s an Australian barmaid opened this door to put the rubbish out and found herself face-to-face with a ghostly disembodied head, which she later identified from a portrait as being that of none other than Oliver Goldsmith.

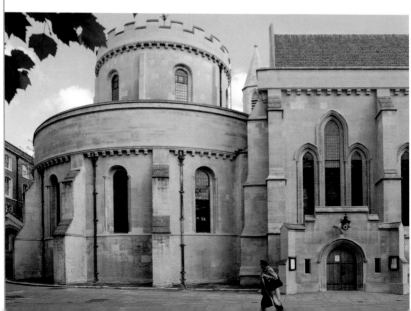

74

7 Backtrack past Goldsmith Buildings, turn right, go through the gate and head left along Fleet Street.

As you pass Temple Bar, the monument in the middle of the road, you leave the City of London and pass into the City of Westminster. Keep ahead until you arrive at The George, a seemingly old English pub that actually dates only from the 1930s, although it stands on older foundations. A ghostly cavalier has been known to terrify staff inside.

8 Cross Strand via the crossing.

To your left is St Clement Danes, reputedly the church of 'Oranges and Lemons' from the nursery rhyme.

ST CLEMENT DANES CHURCH;
OPEN DAILY FOR PRAYERS
www.st-clement-danes.co.uk

9 Go right off the crossing, passing on your left the grandiose Gothic revival buildings of the Royal Courts of Justice, opened in 1882. Pass Temple Bar and go first left into Bell Yard.

It was here that Mrs Lovett once kept her celebrated pie shop. People flocked from all over London to gorge on her tasty wares, oblivious to the fact that the meat was provided by a nearby barber whose name was Sweeney Todd.

10 Backtrack left out of Bell Yard and keep ahead over Chancery Lane. Keep ahead along Fleet Street and

pause outside the church of St Dunstan in the West.

The church clock dates from 1671 and if you manage to arrive on the hour you can enjoy the spectacle of the two giants on either side of it lifting their clubs and making half-hearted attempts to strike the bells, a task they have been performing for more than 300 years.

ST DUNSTAN'S CHURCH;
MON-FRI 11-2 www.stdunstaninthewest.org

11 A little way past the church, turn left into the dark and sinister Hen and Chickens Court.

The creepy courtyard into which you emerge makes the perfect place to contemplate the fact that you're standing behind No. 185 Fleet Street. This is where Sweeney Todd, the Demon Barber of Fleet Street, would cut the throats of unsuspecting customers and then, by way of an underground tunnel, drag their bodies to Bell Yard where Mrs Lovett turned them into tender meat pies for her unsuspecting customers. Sweeney Todd was largely a Victorian creation, so the tales of his exploits shouldn't unnerve you too much. Yet in this quiet courtyard you could mistake a passing shadow for something more sinister.

12 Head back to Fleet Street, go left and left again along Fetter Lane. Keep to its left and on arrival at Holborn, turn left to reach Chancery Lane Underground Station, where this walk ends.

Monks, Murder and Masons

Clerkenwell, London's secret village, may be a trendy media haunt today but it also has a more sinister and crime-ridden history.

Clerkenwell is a quirky little village that clings precariously to a hilltop overlooking the valley of the river Fleet. Having fallen out of fashion in the 1980s its fortunes have enjoyed a resurgence in recent years, and it has become a popular place for media companies to have their offices. Lively wine bars now occupy premises that, not so long ago, were backstreet boozers frequented by decidedly dubious-looking characters. Yet, scratch the surface, and shades of old Clerkenwell can still be glimpsed. On this walk you will pass a pub that has an unusual distinction; gaze in awe upon a medieval gatehouse that Shakespeare would have known; duck into some sinister old alleyways; uncover a former courthouse where Freemasons now bare breast and knee; see a police court that Dickens visited; and end in a secluded courtyard where a gruesome legend will send shivers racing down your spine. Clerkenwell is one of those areas that cast a unique spell that it is easy to fall under. You will certainly want to return.

> Turn left out of Farringdon Station and cross to the Castle Pub.

The Castle has an unusual distinction, which it acquired when the Prince Regent (later George IV) reputedly ran up a huge debt at one of the area's gambling dens. In desperate need of cash, he dropped in at the pub and asked the landlord if he would accept his gold watch as security on a loan. The tavern-keeper didn't recognize his royal visitor, but since the timepiece was obviously worth more than the amount being asked for, he happily obliged. The next day a royal messenger arrived to redeem the pledge and granted the pub a pawnbroker's licence. The pawnbroker's sign of three golden balls still adorns the Castle's exterior and a large painting inside depicts the event.

2 Immediately after the Castle turn left into narrow Faulkener's Alley, a sinister thoroughfare reminiscent of the days when this was one of London's most crime-ridden quarters. It is something of a relief to turn right at the end and ascend the slope of Benjamin Street. The little park on your left was once an overflow graveyard for a nearby church. As the street name changes to Albion Place, keep ahead, then turn left along St John Street and pause before St John's Gate.

Surrounded by featureless office blocks, this impressive edifice dates from 1504 and was once the main entrance to the Priory of the Knights Hospitallers of St John. Following their dissolution it became the Office of the Revels, to which 16th-century dramatists, such as William Shakespeare, would bring their plays to be – or not to be – licensed for public performance. In 1874, the Most Venerable Order of the Hospital of St John of Jerusalem acquired it, and three years later the St John's Ambulance Brigade was founded here. Today, a small museum occupies the old gatehouse and regular tours are given.

ST JOHN'S AMBULANCE MUSEUM;
MON-SAT 10-4 www.sja.org.uk/museum

3 Keep ahead over Clerkenwell Road. Proceed into St John's Square – be sure to peek through the iron gates on the right to glimpse some of the old monastery buildings – then head through narrow Jerusalem Passage in the square's top right corner. At its end look up at the green plaque on the right that commemorates Thomas Britton.

Thomas Britton earned a living by selling coal from his premises on this

DISTANCE 1.75 miles (3km)

ALLOW 1 hour 30 minutes

START Farringdon Underground Station

FINISH Farringdon Underground Station

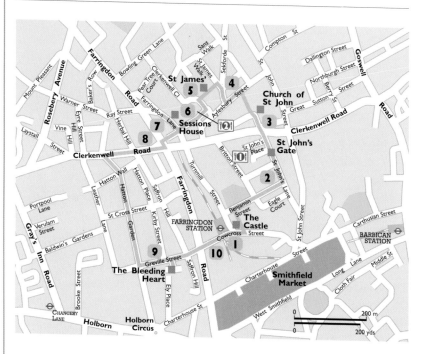

site. But when his day's work was done the 'musical small-coalman' shook off the shackles of a humble tradesman, and entertained 'the most aristocratic company in London' with musical soirees, held in the gloomy room above his shop. Elegant ladies, fashionable beaus and even the composer Handel were among those who thronged here. Britton's death was bizarre. One day he was introduced to a blacksmith named Honeyman, who was a skilled ventriloquist. Knowing that Britton was terrified of ghosts,

Honeyman used his talent to announce 'as if by a supernatural messenger, speaking from a distance…the death of Britton'. The experience so unnerved Britton that he took to his bed and died.

4 Turn left on to Aylesbury Street, right into St James's Walk, left through the gates and cross to St James's Church where, to the right of the steps, is a weatherworn tombstone where the name Steinberg can just about be discerned.

It commemorates Ellen Steinberg and her four children, who were murdered on 8 September 1834. Their killer was Johann Steinberg, Ellen's husband, and, as he then committed suicide, his motive was never ascertained. Ellen and the children were buried at St James's, their tombstone paid for by public subscription. Her husband was buried by night at a nearby crossroads with a stake through his heart, the customary way of dealing with suicidal murderers in the early 19th century.

5 Go past the steps and exit the churchyard via its main gate.

You might like to take a look inside the church, if it is open, to catch a glimpse of the 19th-century iron 'modesty boards' that are strategically placed around the foot of the stairs, intended to prevent gentlemen of the parish from looking up the ladies' skirts.

6 Go left along Clerkenwell Close and right on to Clerkenwell Green, the most singular feature of which is a total absence of greenery. Ahead of you is the former Middlesex Sessions House.

This grandiose building opened in 1782 and by the 19th century had become England's busiest courthouse. By 1919 London's expanding criminal community had outgrown the premises and the courts moved elsewhere. It is now the London Masonic Centre, where the basement cells have been converted into a private bar. As to spirits of a more chilling variety, its plush interior is haunted by two ghosts. On autumn afternoons the flimsy form of a grey lady has been known to float up the staircase adjacent to the main bar, while the clammy presence of an unseen 'something' has also been sensed by several members in a second-floor room.

7 Pass to the right of the Old Sessions House and veer right on to Farringdon Lane and pause for a while at the Clerks Well.

Originally a gathering place for parish clerks, this spring became known as *Fons Clericorum,* from which the name Clerkenwell was derived. Lost for centuries, the well was rediscovered in 1924. It can now be viewed through the windows, as can several information boards giving a detailed history.

8 Backtrack along Farringdon Lane, go right over Vine Street Bridge, left along Farringdon Road, go right at the traffic lights and into Clerkenwell Road. Cross the crossing just before Herbal Hill and proceed into Hatton Garden, the centre of London's jewellery trade since 1836.

No. 54, which you pass on the left, was the former Hatton Garden Police Court where Oliver Twist appeared before the cantankerous magistrate, Mr Fang. Dickens based the character on magistrate Mr Laing, who held court here between 1836 and 1838, and whose courtroom outbursts were infamous. His career ended when Dickens's depiction turned public opinion against him.

9 Take the second left into Greville Street and the first right into Bleeding Heart Yard.

A gruesome legend lies behind this secluded yard's unusual name. On 26

WHERE TO EAT

🍴 THE JERUSALEM TAVERN,
55 Britton Street;
Tel: 020 7490 4281.
With the ambience of an 18th-century coffee house, this tiny pub offers a variety of traditional ales.

🍴 DANS LE NOIR,
30-31 Clerkenwell Green;
Tel: 020 7253 1100.
www.danslenoir.com
If the thought of eating, drinking and chatting in total darkness appeals to you, check out their website for opening times.

January 1662, Lady Elizabeth Hatton was reputedly murdered in the courtyard of her house that stood hereabouts. Some versions of the legend state that her body was torn limb from limb, others that it was never found save for one organ, her heart, which both versions agree was discovered still pumping copious amounts of blood onto the cobblestones of the yard. The fact that no such murder ever took place should not be allowed to stand in the way of such a fanciful legend. The Bleeding Heart Tavern in the yard's right-hand corner positively thrives on whetting customers' appetites with the bloodthirsty tale.

10 Exit right along Greville Street, cross Farringdon Road into Cowcross Street and end at Farringdon Underground Station, on the left.

Burnings and Bodysnatchers

Get a sense of London's vast and extraordinary history, from the days of the Plague and the Great Fire right back to the Peasants' Revolt of 1381.

First stop is a visit to an ancient plague pit, followed by central London's only surviving Tudor townhouse, the walls of which drip with atmosphere. The next section is, to say the least, a little bloodthirsty, as you pass through Europe's largest meat market. A visit to the oldest parish church in London will then transport you back to 1123, and taking the time to absorb its atmosphere is a must. Having crossed the site where executions were once carried out in public, including that of the Scottish patriot Sir William Wallace, you pass by the buildings of London's oldest hospital to still stand on its original site, and arrive at the spot where the Great Fire of London burnt itself out in 1666. Tales of bodysnatchers, ghosts and bloodshed abound in these parts, as do fascinating sights and facts. The walk ends beneath the streets of the modern metropolis, where you can stand among Anglo-Saxon and Roman ruins and view a sinister reminder of the days when even inside a coffin was not a safe place to be!

1 Turn left out of Barbican Underground Station on to Aldersgate Street and go first left into Carthusian Street. Turn right through the gates a little way along and enter Charterhouse Square.

London has suffered many catastrophes, but few compare to the devastation caused by the Black Death of 1348-1349. The epidemic claimed the lives of half of England's population and an even higher proportion of Londoners. The numbers of dead far exceeded the capacity of the capital's burial grounds and new ones were dug and consecrated for mass burials. One such plague pit is still visible on the other side of the square's railings. It was given to the City of London by Norman knight Sir Walter de Manny and thousands of victims were buried here.

2 Continue in an anti-clockwise direction around the square and stop by the huge wooden gates of London's only surviving Tudor townhouse.

This was originally a Carthusian monastery established in 1370. But during the Dissolution of the Monasteries the then prior, John Houghton, invited Thomas Cromwell to the Charterhouse to 'discuss' the issue of Henry VIII's supremacy over the church in England. Cromwell responded by having Houghton sent to the Tower of London. Found guilty of treason he was sentenced to death, and on 4 May 1535, along with several of his fellow monks,

WHERE TO EAT

|O| THE RISING SUN,
38 Cloth Fair;
Tel: 020 7726 6671.
This 18th-century pub is very much a locals' place. Prices are exceptionally good for the area.

|O| THE VIADUCT TAVERN,
126 Newgate Street;
Tel: 020 7606 8476.
A great favourite with lawyers and others who have business at the Old Bailey opposite.

was dragged on a hurdle to Tyburn to be hanged, drawn and quartered. One of Prior Houghton's arms was then nailed to the wooden gates that loom before you to serve as a warning to the remaining monks. In 1547 the buildings were acquired by John Dudley, Duke of Northumberland, possibly as a home for his son, Guildford Dudley, and his wife, Lady Jane Grey. He was executed for his part in proclaiming Lady Jane Grey queen. In 1565 Thomas, 4th Duke of Norfolk, bought the Charterhouse but was executed in 1572 for plotting to marry Mary, Queen of Scots. In 1611 the wealthy Sir Thomas Sutton purchased the building and established a school for boys and a retirement home for men. The school moved out in the 19th century, but the pensioners remain and share their home with the ghost of the Duke of Norfolk who has been known to stride down the main staircase sans head.

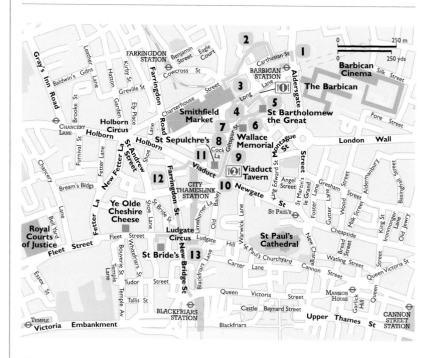

DISTANCE **1 mile (1.6 km)**

ALLOW **1 hour 30 minutes**

START **Barbican Underground Station**

FINISH **Blackfriars Underground Station**

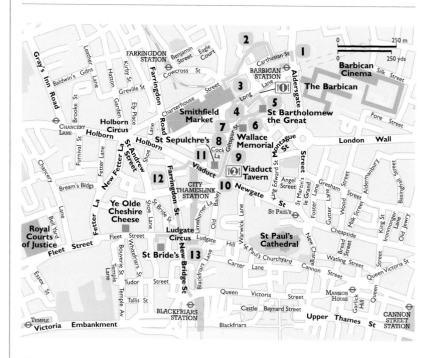

3 Exit the square through the gates. Cross to the left side of Charterhouse Street and go left into Grand Avenue.

You are passing through Europe's largest market, Smithfield Meat Market, designed in 1868 by Sir Horace Jones. Your way is lined with boards giving a detailed history of your surroundings.

4 Keep ahead over the crossing, bear left along Long Lane, first right into Barley Mow Passage, left into Cloth Fair and pause at its junction with Cloth Court.

The tall gabled building predates the Great Fire of London (1666) and gives an glimpse of the medieval city.

5 Continue ahead and go right through the gates to cross the Churchyard of St Bartholomew the Great. Go down the steps in its left corner and enter the church.

St Bartholomew the Great is the oldest parish church in London, founded in 1123 by Rahere. Legend holds that he was the court jester to Henry I and founded a priory here to give thanks to God and St Bartholomew for saving him from death by malaria, which he contracted while in Rome. Rahere's tomb can be seen to the left of the high altar. In June 1866 it was opened and one of his sandals was taken away. This so angered Rahere that his ghost still wanders the church, searching for his missing footwear. Take time to explore this extremely atmospheric church.

ST BARTHOLOMEW' S CHURCH;

TUE-SUN www.greatstbarts.com

6 Exit the church and keep ahead through the old gatehouse. Once on the other side, stop and look up at the structure above. It is one of the oldest surviving timber-framed façades in London and dates from 1595.

In the square outside this gatehouse the Peasants' Revolt of 1381 reached its bloody conclusion when Richard II faced peasant leader Watt Tyler. As Tyler rode up to meet the king, the Lord Mayor of London, William Walworth, stabbed Tyler, who was then dragged into the church and beheaded on a makeshift block.

7 Keep walking ahead. On the left is the memorial to Sir William Wallace, who was executed here in 1348.

This was once a favoured spot for public executions. Poisoners were boiled alive

here and, during the reign of Mary I, Protestants were burnt at the stake. Their ghostly cries of agony are sometimes said to be heard early in the morning.

8 Continue ahead past the Wallace Memorial. Keep ahead into Giltspur Street, cross to its right side, to the junction with Cock Lane.

The Golden Boy or Fat Boy who looks down at you from the wall marks the spot where the Great Fire of London burnt itself out in 1666. Londoners reasoned that since the fire began at Pudding Lane and finished at Pye Corner, it was God's punishment for gluttony. Hence the inscription beneath, that states he was put up in memory of the 'Late fire of London occasioned by the sin of Gluttony...'

9 Continue on Giltspur Street to the old watch house by the iron gates.

It dates from 1791 and was built to accommodate a night watchman whose job was to protect the churchyard beyond the railings from raids by bodysnatchers.

10 When you get to the traffic lights cross to visit the Viaduct Tavern.

This exquisite pub was opened in 1875 and has some wonderful silvered mirrors and decorated glass. On the wall to the right as you enter is a painting of three ladies, representing agriculture, banking and the arts. 'Art' still bears the scars of an encounter with a drunken soldier in World War I who stabbed her in the back with his bayonet. The tavern is the most haunted pub in the City of London.

11 Leave the pub, cross Giltspur Street and pause to admire St Sepulchre's Church.

The bells used to ring out to announce executions at Newgate Prison, which once stood opposite the Viaduct Tavern. The site is now occupied by the Central Criminal Courts or Old Bailey. These same bells were also the bells of Old Bailey that asked: "When will you pay me?" in the nursery rhyme *Oranges and Lemons*. A history of the church can be read on the board by its door.

ST SEPULCHRE'S CHURCH;

www.st-sepulchre.org.uk

12 Keep ahead over Snow Hill, cross to the left side of Holborn Viaduct at the crossing, and descend the stairs just after Gresham House. Bear left along Farringdon Street and keep ahead over Turnagain Lane; go over the crossing by Bear Alley. Veer left over Stonecutter Street and keep ahead to turn right at the traffic lights on to Fleet Street. Cross to its left side and take the second left into St Bride's Avenue.

The spire that rises over you is one of Sir Christopher Wren's most beautiful and is known as the 'wedding cake spire' because the modern wedding cake is based on its tiered structure. Wren rebuilt the church of St Bride's after the Great Fire of London, although his structure was destroyed in the Blitz and also had

to be rebuilt. Bombs revealed remains of buildings on the site that date back to Roman times. These are reached by turning right as you enter and descending the steps into the crypt. Also worth looking at is the very rusty iron coffin, which can be viewed at the far end of the first passage you encounter at the foot of the stairs. This was intended to prevent the body within from being stolen by bodysnatchers. Unfortunately, since iron took longer to decay than wood, churches charged a premium for such burials and so the iron coffin never really caught on.

ST BRIDE'S CHURCH; www.stbrides.com

13 Having explored the crypt, backtrack along Fleet Street, go right at the traffic lights and keep ahead along New Bridge Street to Blackfriars Underground Station, where this walk ends.

The Splendour of St Paul's

The area around St Paul's Cathedral has much to offer those willing to leave behind the busy main roads and explore its timeless alleyways.

This walk takes you from the bustle of Blackfriars into a warren of backstreets that are still laid out along their medieval patterns. It dips in and out of churchyards where the numbers of burials have actually raised them above the level of the streets. There's opportunity to venture inside St Paul's Cathedral, where you can marvel at its splendour while searching for its ghostly clergyman. The historical figures we meet in the course of this stroll are as diverse as they are fascinating. William Shakespeare and Queen Isabella are just two of the names you will come across as you take in the sights at the heart of the historic City. But it is the variety of sights encountered that make this a memorable walk. An old church where a ghostly bell has been known to ring out in the early hours; a lovely old park where a wall of tiles remembers long-ago acts of heroism; a creepy wall where a sinister black dog appears on moonless nights; and a city institution where workers have encountered supernatural activity.

| Turn right out of exit 1 at Blackfriars Station, go left at the Blackfriar Pub and walk along Queen Victoria Street to take the first left into Blackfriars Lane. Go right into Playhouse Yard – named for the Blackfriars theatre in which Shakespeare was a shareholder – and keep ahead into the paved alleyway.

On the left is one of the City's oldest burial grounds. Its level has been raised by the enormous number of burials that took place here in the 18th and 19th centuries. A crumbling section of wall can be seen on the right at the top of the steps. This is a surviving fragment from the Priory of the Dominicans, which stood here from the 13th to the 15th century when it was closed under the Dissolution of the Monasteries.

2 Keep ahead to pass the Cockpit Pub (the interior of which is built to resemble a cock-fighting den) and go right down St Andrew's Hill where immediately on the left is the church of St Andrew-by-the-Wardrobe.

The wardrobe in question was the King's Wardrobe, a building that stood to the north of the church: clothing and furnishings for the royal household were kept there until it was destroyed in the Great Fire of London in 1666. William Shakespeare lived in the parish for 15 years and owned a house in nearby Ireland Yard. A memorial window to St Andrew's most famous parishioner can be seen inside the church. St Andrew's possesses three bells which were

transferred here in 1933 from Avenbury church in Herefordshire. One of them, Gabriel, was reputed to ring of its own accord whenever a vicar of Avenbury died: it is said to have done so shortly after its arrival, when its mournful knell woke local residents in the dead of one night. Next morning word arrived that, at the moment when the bell had rung, the incumbent at Avenbury had died.

3 Backtrack and head up St Andrew's Hill to go right on to Carter Lane. Take the first right into Wardrobe Place to view its robust 18th-century houses and absorb its peaceful ambience. Exit and go right along Carter Lane, first left in to Deans Court and cross St Paul's Churchyard to get to St Paul's Cathedral.

The white statue that looks away from the cathedral is of Queen Anne – she was the reigning monarch when this, the fifth cathedral dedicated to St Paul to stand

DISTANCE **2 miles (3.2km)**

ALLOW **1 hour 30 minutes**

START **Blackfriars Underground Station, Exit 1**

FINISH **St Paul's Underground Station**

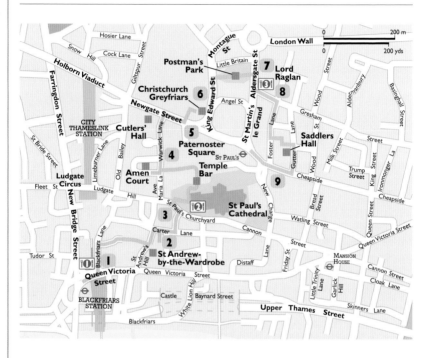

on this site, opened. Enter the cathedral via the door on the left and pause by the Kitchener Memorial Chapel on the left. Witnesses have reported seeing a ghostly, whistling clergyman who glides across the chapel and melts into the wall.

ST PAUL'S CATHEDRAL;

MON-SAT 8.30-4 www.stpauls.co.uk

4 Exit the cathedral, turn right and cross to Temple Bar. For more than 200 years the daily life of London passed through this old gateway. From the 17th

to the 19th century it stood at the junction of Fleet Street and Strand, where the Cities of London and Westminster meet. A full history can be read on the information board. Pass through Temple Bar into Paternoster Square, turn left, and keep ahead over Ave Maria Lane. Bear right, then go left past Amen Corner to pause by the gates into Amen Court.

The buildings that line its right side date to the 1680s. Behind the bushes at the

far end of the court there is a dark wall, behind which Newgate Prison stood until the early 20th century. On the other side of the wall there was once a passage known as Deadman's Walk, so called because prisoners walked along it to their execution and were buried beneath it afterwards. The wall is haunted by the Black Dog of Newgate, described as a shapeless black mass that slithers along the top of the wall, slides into the courtyard and then melts away. Legend holds that its origins date back to the reign of Henry III when the prisoners at Newgate resorted to cannibalism during a famine. One of their victims was a sorcerer who had been imprisoned there. Retribution followed swiftly in the form of a hideous black dog that killed those responsible and then returned to haunt Newgate Prison.

5 Backtrack to Amen Corner and go left along Ave Maria Lane, which changes to Warwick Lane. Keep ahead over Warwick Square, go past Cutlers Hall where you can look up at its terracotta frieze by Sheffield sculptor

Benjamin Creswick (1853-1946), showing cutlers working at their craft. Go right along Newgate Street and cross cautiously to its lefthand side. Go next left and then right through the gates to enter the burial ground of Christchurch Greyfriars.

A few scattered tombs can be glimpsed and if you look underneath the benches you will see that they stand on burial vaults. Queen Isabella, who had her husband Edward II murdered in 1327, was buried in 1358 in the precincts of what was then the Greyfriars Monastery. Her beautiful but angry ghost roams the churchyard on misty autumn mornings.

6 Keep ahead through the churchyard, exit through the gates and turn left then right through the gates that lead through the bombed-out remains of Christchurch Greyfriars. Once through the lovely garden turn left along King Edward Street. Keep ahead past the statue of postal pioneer Sir Roland Hill, cross the crossing and bear right to enter Postman's Park.

Note the number of tombstones that line the walls of the park on either side, remnants from the days when this was one of London's largest burial grounds. Beneath a canopy to the left is the national memorial to heroic men and women, a wall that commemorates those who died saving the lives of others. People like 'William Drake who lost his life in averting a serious accident to a Lady in Hyde Park…'

7 Exit Postman's Park through the opposite gates. Cross over Aldersgate Street, bear right and walk to the Lord Raglan pub, which dates back to 1855.

A phantom girl has been seen in the upstairs bar near the games tables, while a ghostly Roman soldier has been known to cower in a corner of the pub's cellar. Add in the whispering that some customers have said they've heard and it soon becomes obvious that the pub's spirits aren't just kept behind the bar.

8 Turn left out of the Lord Raglan pub, go left on to Gresham Street, turn first right into Foster Lane, keep ahead over Carey Lane, and a little further along squeeze left into the darkly sinister Rose and Crown Court. Follow the passage as it twists right then left (through the railings on the right you will glimpse the courtyard of Saddlers Hall), and as it emerges on to Gutter Lane, go right and pause by Saddlers Hall, home to the Worshipful Company of Saddlers.

WHERE TO EAT

[O] THE BLACKFRIAR,
174 Queen Victoria Street;
Tel: 020 7236 5474.
Enjoy a drink while admiring the Arts and Crafts mosaics on the walls.
Be warned – it gets very crowded.

[O] CRYPT CAFÉ,
St Paul's Cathedral, St Paul's Churchyard;
Tel: 020 7236 4128.
Down in the crypt of St Paul's, a nice place to enjoy a sandwich and a tea or coffee while resting your feet.

[O] THE LORD RAGLAN,
61 St Martin's le Grand;
Tel: 020 7726 4756.
Closed weekends. Cavernous interior. Very much a locals' pub with good food at reasonable prices.

Rebuilt after bomb damage in World War II, this is the fourth hall to stand on the site. People have complained of the nauseous smell of decaying flesh in the basement area, while jangling keys, slamming doors and inexplicable thunderous bangs are among the other paranormal phenomena that people have experienced within the walls of this venerable city building.

9 Continue to the end of Gutter Lane. Go right along Cheapside and arrive at St Paul's Underground Station, where this walk ends.

Ghosts of the Old City

City workers hurry past with barely a glance at their surroundings but a slower pace reveals the area's history, from Roman times to the present.

This walk explores some of the capital's most intriguing places. Stately churches cower behind monstrous office blocks as though terrified of being spotted, demolished and their sites turned into another unsightly temple to Mammon. The area has two of Sir Christopher Wren's grandest church towers, not to mention a pub he is reputed to have built for the workmen at St Paul's Cathedral. From here you will make your way to a mysterious Roman Temple, one of the few artefacts from the early history of the city to be still visible above street level. Having contemplated its origins you descend a narrow street to arrive at the beautiful exterior of an old city church inside which a mummified corpse still resides. You will pass the site of the house of Dick Whittington, and the hidden city hostelry that was once home to successive Lord Mayors of London. Finally, you will ponder one of London's most enigmatic relics, the London Stone, the origins and purpose of which can only be guessed at.

Turn right from the cathedral exit of St Paul's Underground Station and keep ahead over New Change into Cheapside. This largely uninspiring thoroughfare is named for the fact that it was once the City's main market place. Keep going until you arrive at the Church of St Mary le Bow.

There has been a church on this site since the 11th century, although earlier buildings appear to have enjoyed a less than harmonious existence. A series of unfortunate events led to a general consensus that the building was cursed. In 1090 the church roof was blown off during a storm and the falling debris caused considerable loss of life. In 1196 William Fitzosbert took sanctuary inside the church tower and the resultant attempt to smoke him out caused severe damage. In 1271 the tower collapsed killing 20 passersby. In 1284 Lawrence Duckett, a goldsmith, was murdered inside the church. In reprisal 16 men were hanged and one woman was burnt at the stake. The church was destroyed in the Great Fire of 1666 and Wren rebuilt it, since when it has enjoyed a relatively curse-free existence – that is, if you exclude destruction by bombing in World War II. To be a true cockney you must be born within the sound of this church's bells, the same Bow bells that urged the runaway Dick Whittington to 'turn again' and be Lord Mayor of London. The bells were silenced following bomb damage in World War II and remained mute for 20 years until being restored in 1961. Technically, therefore, no cockneys could

have been born during this period.
MON-FRI www.stmarylebow.co.uk

2 Turn right along Bow Lane and keep ahead until you arrive at Groveland Court on the right. Here you will find Williamson's Tavern.

The tavern stands on the site of the London mansion of Sir John Oldcastle, who inspired Shakespeare to create the character of Falstaff. Later, this site became home to successive Lord Mayors of London until they moved to the Mansion House in 1752. William III and Queen Mary once visited and presented the splendid wrought-iron

DISTANCE **1.25 miles (2km)**

ALLOW **1 hour 20 minutes**

START **St Paul's Underground Station**

FINISH **Cannon Street Station**

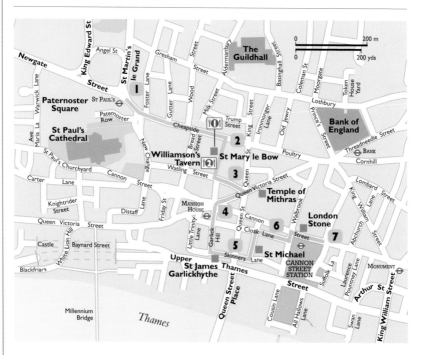

gates that you can still see at the far side of the courtyard. In the 18th century the Williamson family bought the property and turned it into a hotel, which proved popular with clergymen visiting nearby St Paul's Cathedral. The current building was built in the 1930s by William Hollis Junior, who was driven out by the ghost that is said to haunt the premises. Several barmaids have refused to work evenings because of ghostly activity and there are tales of police dog handlers struggling to persuade their canine charges to enter

the alleyway, so terrified are they of something they can see or sense within.

3 Exit right from Groveland Court, continue along Bow Lane and turn left along Watling Street. Ye Olde Watling Pub on the corner is said to have been built by Sir Christopher Wren to accommodate the labourers of St Paul's Cathedral. Keep ahead, past the statue of the Cordwainer – a maker of fancy shoes – recalling medieval days when Bow Lane was known as

Cordwainer Street. Keep ahead over Queen Street, bear right over Queen Victoria Street, turn left and go up the steps to the remains of the Roman Temple of Mithras.

Discovered in 1954 during construction work on nearby Walbrook, this temple to the sun and the Persian god of light was uprooted to its present site and reconstructed on a platform some six feet above street level. Hence, much of the mysticism of what would have been a subterranean temple has inevitably been lost. Mithraism became popular throughout the Roman Empire in the 2nd century. However, following the Empire's acceptance of Christianity in the 4th century, the temple was abandoned, apparently in haste. The remains show the Roman influence on the design of Christian churches, featuring a central nave, side aisles and a rounded apse. A history can be read on the railings.

4 Go back down the steps, turn left along Queen Victoria Street, left at the lights, cross Cannon Street, bear right and then left down Garlick Hill to the Church of St James Garlickhythe.

Christopher Wren rebuilt this church in 1683 and its steeple is one of the most graceful in the City of London. Its interior is well worth a visit and handheld history boards are available. Sadly the church's most distinguished resident is no longer on view. In 1855 during clearance of the vicar's vault, the mummified corpse of a young man was discovered. He was put on public display inside the church and became a familiar fixture for generations of parishioners, who named him Jimmy Garlick. Impish choir boys would sometimes place a ruff around his neck and sit him in the choir stalls. Today he is kept in a cabinet well away from prying eyes, although his may be the skeletal spectre that has appeared to some visitors.

CHURCH OF ST JAMES GARLICKHYTHE;
MON-FRI 10.30-4, PLUS SUN SERVICES
www.stjamesgarlickhythe.org.uk

5 Go along Skinners Lane to the left of the church. Keep ahead into College Street and turn first left up College Hill. The church on your right is St Michael Paternoster Royal.

The church was rebuilt in 1409 by Sir Richard Whittington – the pantomime character Dick Whittington is loosely based on him – who also founded the College of St Spirit and St Mary, from which College Hill takes its name. When Whittington died in 1423 he was buried in the church. However, during the reign of Edward VI, the rector Thomas Mountain opened his tomb, anticipating vast treasure. Finding none, he ripped off the corpse's leaden sheet in a fit of pique. When Mary I came to the throne the cantankerous cleric was removed from office and Whittington's remains were re-shrouded, although his whereabouts are no longer known.

6 Continue along College Hill, passing on the right the blue plaque that marks the site of Dick Whittington's mansion. Go first right along Cloak Lane, left on to Dowgate Hill, right along Cannon Street, cross to its left side and pause outside No. 111 where, encased in glass behind an ornate metal grille, you will find the London Stone.

The origins of this curious relic are lost in the mists of time. It has been suggested that it was once part of a ritualistic or sacrificial druidic altar or stone circle. The most popular theory, however, is that it was a Roman milestone – possibly

WHERE TO EAT

🍴 **THE PLACE BELOW,**
St Mary le Bow Church, Cheapside;
Tel: 020 7329 0789.
www.theplacebelow.co.uk
In what is, perhaps, one of the most unique settings of any City restaurant, this eatery offers delicious homemade quiches, salads, soup and a hot dish of the day.

🍴 **WILLIAMSON'S TAVERN,**
1 Groveland Court, Off Bow Lane;
Tel: 020 7248 5750.
A good selection of beers and a menu of hearty pub fare make the tavern a favourite with local workers.

the one from which all distances in the province of Britannia were measured. Throughout the Middle Ages the stone stood in the middle of Cannon Street and was much larger than the fragment that survives today. It was the symbolic heart of the City of London, over which oaths were sworn and deals struck. The renowned occultist Dr John Dee (1527-1608), who lived close by, was particularly fascinated by it and is rumoured to have stolen it in order to use chippings in his alchemy experiments. Today it goes unnoticed by the majority of passersby, a curious though intriguing remnant of bygone London.

7 Cross back over Cannon Street to Cannon Street Station, where this walk ends.

WALK

15

Remnants of Rome

Soaring office blocks hardly seem conducive to delving into the past but this walk will show you what lies beneath the pavements of London.

This walk begins outside the Museum of London. If you make time to go inside before you set off, you'll see several artefacts that have been discovered at sites along the walk. Within a few steps of leaving the modern museum building you will have descended a flight of stairs and found yourself staring up at an impressive bastion of Roman London. The walk then follows sections of the old city wall that were uncovered by the bombs of the Blitz. The Roman remains that you gaze upon are still extremely impressive and it is easy to see why the waves of invaders that arrived long after the Romans had departed came to the conclusion that these places must have been built by mythical giants from the distant past. You will also step inside the church where John Milton (1608-1674), author of *Paradise Lost*, was buried – and learn of the gruesome fate that befell his body 119 years after his death. The walk ends beneath the Guildhall Art Gallery at the remains of the City's Roman amphitheatre.

Turn left outside the Museum of London and pass the memorial to John Wesley's Evangelical conversion, which occurred near here. The full story is detailed on a plaque. Keep ahead along Bastion High Walk and go left by No. 140 to descend the stone stairs to the right. On arrival at the lowest level keep ahead towards the stone tower.

On the wall opposite, to the right, a board gives the history of this section of the London Wall. Scramble up the earth bank to the left and look up at the sturdy Roman bastion that looms over you. This is the northern tower from the west gate of the Roman fort, built in AD 120. It was only rediscovered after the Blitz had reduced this area to rubble and subsequent excavations to build the soaring residential, cultural and office complex that surrounds you revealed this magnificent piece of masonry.

2 Keep ahead past the brick wall then cross right to the railings. Beyond stands the hall of the Worshipful Company of Barbers who have occupied the site since the 1440s, although the current building dates from 1969.

Bygone barbers also practised surgery and bloodletting. In 1540 they were amalgamated with the Surgeons Guild and granted an annual allocation of four bodies from the public executioner for experimentation. On 24 November 1740, a 16-year-old boy named William Duell was hanged at Tyburn and his body was brought to the hall. As it was

WHERE TO EAT

|O| WATERSIDE CAFÉ,
Level 0, Barbican Centre;
Tel: 020 7638 4141.
A very busy self-service café offering filling meals and light snacks. Sit inside or, if you can find a table, on the lakeside terrace and watch the world go by.

|O| OLD DR BUTLERS HEAD,
2 Masons Avenue;
Tel: 020 7606 3504.
A panelled interior, gas lights that barely illuminate, and an ambience that can only be described as Dickensian in a pub tucked away down an alleyway close to Guildhall.

being prepared for dissection he suddenly gasped and came back to life. He was returned to Newgate Prison and his sentence was reduced to transportation. The barbers and surgeons went their separate ways in 1800, the latter decamping to their own premises in Holborn. A ghostly Roman soldier seen in the basement is just one of several phantoms that appear inside the building. The herb garden to the left, within the Roman wall, is worth exploring.

3 Exit the herb garden and swerve right round the wall to look up at the raised mound on top of which you can see several tombstones. This was part of the old burial ground of St Giles Cripplegate where victims of the 1665

DISTANCE **2 miles (3.2km)**

ALLOW **2 hours**

START **Outside the main entrance of the Museum of London**

FINISH **Bank Underground Station**

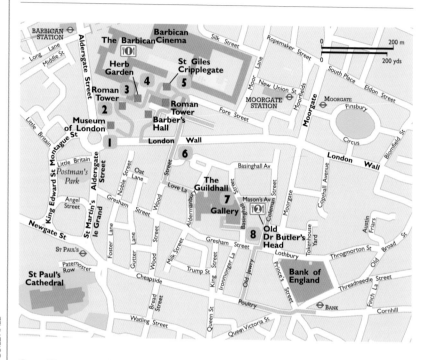

Great Plague were buried. On arrival at the lake, follow the flagstone path to its right. As it veers right a plaque details the history of the 13th-century St Giles Cripplegate tower ahead of you. Follow the path right and cross to the green gates through which the massive tower can be admired. Backtrack to the west gate's northern tower. Go down the steps, turn left, ascend the slope and go left along London Wall. Turn left into Wood Street and first right into St Alphage Garden.

Keep ahead and go left into the lovely garden which was formerly the site of a church named for St Alfege, the 29th Archbishop of Canterbury, who was beaten to death by Vikings at Greenwich in 1012. The church's history can be read on a board to the right. Ahead of you is an impressive section of the old Roman Wall. In April 1907, a reader wrote to the *City Press* to complain that as he was passing this wall one night an arm had reached out and barred his passage. He turned away in shock and when he

summoned the courage to look round a dark figure was striding towards the wall. It kept walking and then melted into the brickwork.

4 Leave the gardens, go left and cross to the righthand side of the covered parking area.

Looking through the ugly concrete fence in the corner you can view the soaring ruin of the 14th-century tower of the chapel of the Priory of St Elsing Spital, founded in 1329 as a hospital for the blind. A history of it can be read on the railings. Again, this was rediscovered when the surrounding area was destroyed by bombing in World War II.

5 Backtrack to Wood Street, turn right, cross to its left side and bear left into St Giles' Terrace. Go left at the childcare centre and cross to the railings where another section of the wall is visible along with a history tablet. Walk clockwise around the church of St Giles Cripplegate to enter its main door.

Inside the church, cross to the opposite side where a display details the devastation caused to this area by the Blitz. One photograph shows the toppled statue of the poet John Milton (1608-1674) lying among the rubble. The statue, which dates from 1904, now stands against the wall a little way behind you. Walk over and stand before him. Milton was buried in the church when he died in 1674. His grave was opened in 1793 and an attempt was made to pull

out his teeth. This being unsuccessful, a bystander picked up a stone and loosened them with a blow. They were taken away as souvenirs by several onlookers, along with a rib bone and handfuls of his hair. The caretaker, Elizabeth Grant, then charged sixpence for people to view the body. No wonder the face of Milton's statue wears a look of disapproval. Other famous figures associated with the church include Oliver Cromwell (1599-1658), who was married here in 1620.

CHURCH OF ST GILES CRIPPLEGATE;
MON-FRI 10-4 www.stgilescripplegate.org.uk

6 Exit the church and backtrack along Wood Street to cross London Wall and keep ahead into the continuation of Wood Street. Go left along Love Lane, right along Aldermanbury, cross to its left side and, just after the administrative buildings of the Guildhall, go left through the barrier and into the courtyard in front of the splendid façade of the Guildhall, built between 1411 and 1430.

Enter the Guildhall through the doors to the left of the barrier. Once inside, look back at the two giants that leer down at you from their perch above the entrance. On the right is Gog and on the left, Magog. They represent warriors in the legendary conflict between ancient Britons and Trojan invaders. The struggle led to the founding of New Troy on the site of which London is said to stand. Several notable trials have been held here and a tablet on the left wall gives details of some of them. They include Lady Jane Grey, the nine-day queen, who was tried

for high treason and then sentenced to death here in 1554.

GUILDHALL; OPEN REGULARLY

www.cityoflondon.gov.uk

7 Exit Guildhall into the main courtyard and go left to enter the Guildhall Art Gallery.

When the foundations for this building were being excavated the remnants of the Roman amphitheatre were discovered. Left in situ, the eastern entrance can now be visited inside the gallery.

GUILDHALL ART GALLERY; DAILY

www.guildhall-art-gallery.org.uk

8 Leave the gallery, go left and left again through Guildhall Buildings. Turn left along Basinghall Street and a little way along go right along the easily missed Mason's Avenue. The timbered neo-Tudor style buildings that line its left

side actually date from 1928. Towards its end on the right is the Old Dr Butler's Head pub which occupies two early 19th-century buildings. The Doctor Butler in question was the court physician to King James 1, a man who devised some decidedly unconventional treatments for his patients. His 'cure' for epilepsy was to fire pistols behind his unsuspecting patient to scare the condition out of them, whilst those suffering with plague would find themselves plunged into ice-cold water. He also brewed a medicinal ale which was only available at taverns that displayed his head on their signs, a practice that this tavern's name remembers. Continue to the end of Mason's Avenue and go right onto Coleman Street. At its end continue into Old Jewry, at the end turn left along Poultry and arrive at Bank Underground Station, where this walk ends.

Jack the Ripper's Trail

Follow in the brutal murderer's footsteps as you trace his spine-chilling progress through Victorian London's notoriously sinister East End.

Over a ten-week period between 31 August and 9 November 1888 five prostitutes – Mary Nichols, Annie Chapman, Elizabeth Stride, Catherine Eddowes and Mary Kelly – were brutally murdered in the East End of London. The ferocity of the mutilations increased with each killing. The police appeared helpless against the killer and the whole of London felt threatened. At the height of the panic a letter was sent to a London news agency purporting to come from the murderer and taunting the police over their inability to catch him. It was signed Jack the Ripper and when it was made public in October 1888 it turned five sordid East End murders into an international phenomenon and elevated the unknown miscreant into the realm of legend. This walk visits three of the murder sites, as well as that of another – which although not thought to be the work of Jack the Ripper, was classed as a Whitechapel Murder, the official name of the police file on which the killings were included.

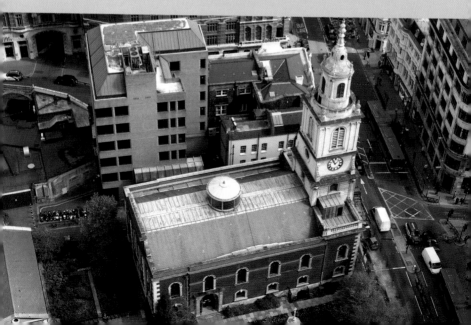

1 From the station turn right on to Aldgate High Street.

At 8.30pm on 29 September 1888 Police Constable Robinson arrested Catherine Eddowes here for being drunk and disorderly. He took her to nearby Bishopsgate Police Station where she was placed in a cell and left to sober up. She was released at 1am the next morning.

2 Continue ahead passing the church of St Botolph, which in 1888 was known as the Prostitutes' Church because the Victorian street walkers plied their trade alongside it.

Go past the church, over the first crossing, swerve right over the second crossing, bear right past the Sir John Cass Foundation School – note the figures of the charity boy and girl in the first-floor alcoves. Turn left into St James's Passage. This was known as Church Passage in 1888. It was here at 1.30am on 30 September 1888 that Joseph Lawende

saw a man and woman talking. Although the woman had her back to him he later identified Catherine Eddowes's clothing, when shown it at a police station, as being the clothes worn by the woman. It is probable that Lawende saw the face of Jack the Ripper.

3 Continue into Mitre Square and cross to the flowerbed.

At 1.45am on 30 September 1888 PC Watkins turned into the square and discovered the mutilated body of Catherine Eddowes on this spot.

4 Turn your back on the flowerbed, head diagonally left across the square and pass through the covered Mitre Passage. Bear right across Creechurch Place, right along Creechurch Lane, go over Bevis Marks and cross Houndsditch into Stoney Lane. Bear right then left into Gravel Lane and go over Middlesex Street. As you do so you leave the City of London and enter

DISTANCE **2.5 miles (4km)**

ALLOW **I hour 45 minutes**

START **Aldgate Underground Station**

FINISH **Aldgate East Underground Station**

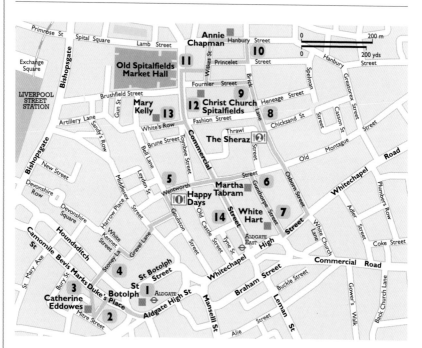

the East End. Keep ahead along New Goulston Street; at the end go left into Goulston Street.

The solid block of flats on its right side is Wentworth Model Dwellings, built in 1886 and largely occupied by Jewish tradesmen in 1888. It was in the doorway, now the takeaway counter of the Happy Days Fish Restaurant, that PC Alfred Long discovered a piece of Catherine Eddowes's apron at 2.55am on 30 September 1888. It was smeared with blood and the killer had evidently used it to clean his hands. The discovery suggests that the murderer lived in the area, since he headed east from Mitre Square and was undoubtedly going to ground. The doorway also contained a sinister chalked message that read, 'The Juwes are the men that will not be blamed for nothing.' The Metropolitan Police, worried that this message might provoke an outbreak of anti-Semitic unrest in the area, erased the graffiti before any photographs could be taken of it.

5 Continue and go right along Wentworth Street. Cross Commercial Street and pause outside the Princess Alice Pub.

In the early days of the hunt for the Ripper, local prostitutes spoke of a man they had nicknamed Leather Apron, who had threatened them near this pub.

6 Continue along Wentworth Street. Turn right into Gunthorpe Street.

The red brick building a little way along on the right stands on the site of George Yard Buildings, where the body of Martha Tabram was found at 5am on 7 August 1888. She had been stabbed 39 times. Some experts maintain that she was the first victim of Jack the Ripper.

7 Continue the length of Gunthorpe Street, passing the White Hart Pub.

A board on the wall gives a brief history of the the Ripper's crimes and suspects. They include George Chapman, a Polish

barber/surgeon who in 1890 worked in a barber's shop in the basement of this pub. Chapman was executed in 1903 for poisoning three of his wives. Inspector Abberline, who headed the search for Jack the Ripper in the area, believed that he may also have been the Ripper.

8 Go through the arch to turn left along Whitechapel High Street. Keep ahead to the traffic lights and go left into Osborn Street. Continue ahead into Brick Lane and pause at its junction with Thrawl Street.

This now leads to a modern council estate but in 1888 it was lined with lodging houses. Mary Nichols was ejected from No. 18 in the early hours of 31 August 1888 because she lacked fourpence to pay for a bed. At 3.40am her body was found a quarter of a mile away in Bucks Row. Her throat had been cut and she had been disembowelled. She spent some of her final hours in the Frying Pan Pub, which is now the Sheraz Indian restaurant on the corner here. However, if you look up at the gable you will see two crossed frying pans and the pub's name, Ye Frying Pan, in brick relief.

9 Continue along Brick Lane and go second left into Fournier Street. The houses here were built in the 18th century for the Huguenot master silk weavers. Go right along Wilkes Street and right into Princelet Street.

The street is lined with 18th-century houses. No. 19 on the left became the

United Friends Synagogue in 1870, and is the oldest minor synagogue in the East End. It is sometimes open to visitors.

www.19princeletstreet.org.uk

10 Turn left on to Brick Lane and go left into Hanbury Street. Its left side is little changed since 1888. The right side was demolished in the 1960s and replaced with the ugly brown brick complex that lines it today.

Pause on the opposite side of the road to No. 30. This is the approximate site of the original No. 29, in the backyard of which the body of Annie Chapman was discovered at 6am on 8 September 1888.

11 Keep ahead along Hanbury Street, pausing by Christchurch Hall on its left side where a board gives a detailed history. Go left along Wilkes Street, right through Puma Court, noting the almshouses on the right which were built in 1860. Turn left on to Commercial Street to the Ten Bells Pub.

Annie Chapman was seen drinking here at 5am on the morning of her murder. A man popped his head round the door and called her out. Mary Kelly, the Ripper's final victim, also frequented the Ten Bells.

12 Keep ahead over Fournier Street. Look up at the soaring tower of Christ Church Spitalfields (1729).

This magnificent church rears over the older streets of Spitalfields, dominating its surroundings. It was designed by Nicholas

WHERE TO EAT

[O] HAPPY DAYS FISH RESTAURANT, 44 Goulston Street;
Tel: 020 7377 9815.
www.happydaysrestaurant.co.uk
The best fish and chips in the area.

[O] THE SHERAZ RESTAURANT, 13 Brick Lane;
Tel: 020 7247 5755.
www.sheraz.co.uk
Great curry and very friendly.

Hawksmoor (1661-1736) and is truly spectacular inside.

CHRIST CHURCH SPITALFIELDS;
SUN 1-4, TUE 11-4 AND AT OTHER TIMES
www.christchurchspitalfields.org.uk

13 Cross Commercial Street via the crossing, bear right and then, just after the White's Row car park, go left through the barrier.

This was once Dorset Street, one of the most crime-ridden streets in the East End of London. Just past the iron steps on the right, a gap in the kerbstones marks the approximate site of Miller's Court, the place where Mary Kelly, Jack the Ripper's final victim, rented a room. Her virtually skinned body was found here on 9 November 1888.

14 Backtrack to Commercial Street, turn right and walk to its end, where you will find Aldgate East Underground Station.

Lore and Legend in Wapping

Tales of ghosts, murders, pirates and executions all combine to make this a journey of discovery in the heart of London's historic dockside area.

Wapping is the first riverside hamlet in the East End of London, and its history is indelibly linked with the sea. Pirates were executed here; smugglers and cut-throats lurked in dingy alleys, some of which survive unchanged. The pubs once echoed with the banter of sailors, while characters as diverse as Captain Bligh and the artist Joseph Turner have lived here. The walk mines this rich seam of history, beginning with a reminder of one of the most famous East End events of the 20th century – the battle of Cable Street – and then explores the circumstances behind a series of gruesome 19th-century murders that caused terror in the area. Having passed through the cavernous interior of Tobacco Dock it takes you past riverside passages and pubs steeped in the ambience of days long gone. A highlight of this section is the opportunity to explore some of the sinister little pathways that lead down to the River Thames from Wapping High Street. It ends with a visit to London's oldest riverside pub.

From Shadwell station turn left along Watney Street. Go over the zebra crossing, bear left and then right into Cable Street. Cross to its left side and keep ahead past the town hall, after which go left through the gates.

On the left is a huge wall painting of the battle of Cable Street, which took place on Sunday 5 October 1936. Sir Oswald Mosley's Fascists were planning to march through the East End taking in Cable Street en route. But the local residents, Jews and Irish Catholics, banded together with various left-wing parties and built barricades in Cable Street to stop them. Fighting broke out between locals and the police. The Home Office, realizing the consequences if the Fascists succeeded in marching along Cable Street, ordered Mosley to cancel the event.

2 Keep ahead through the gates and follow the path as it bends right. Pass on to the earth path to the right of the line of gravestones and cross the lawn to pass through the gate to the left of the church of St George-in-the-East.

Be sure to look at the macabre gravestone by the wall with its crudely carved skull and crossbones. Walk clockwise round the church and pass through the old tower to view the modern interior. The church was designed by Nicholas Hawksmoor and completed in 1723. It was badly damaged in the Blitz with only the outer walls and tower surviving. The new chapel was built within the remains and the two blend harmoniously. If the

church is open you can read a full history on the board inside.
CHURCH SERVICES WED 1.05, SUN 10.15

3 Backtrack through the tower, go down the steps and exit through the gates on to Cannon Street Road. The traffic lights to your right stand on the crossroads where John Williams was buried by night with a stake driven through his heart.

On Saturday 7 December 1811 Timothy Marr and three members of his family, together with their shop boy, were found brutally murdered in the linen-drapers shop he ran at 29 Ratcliffe Highway (now simply the Highway). On 19 December an identical crime took place at the King's Arms in New Gravel Lane, when publican John Williamson, his wife and barmaid were murdered in an equally gruesome manner. Suspicion fell on John Williams, a young sailor who was

DISTANCE **3.5 miles (5.6km)**

ALLOW **2 hours**

START **Shadwell Docklands Light Railway Station**

FINISH **Wapping Underground Station**

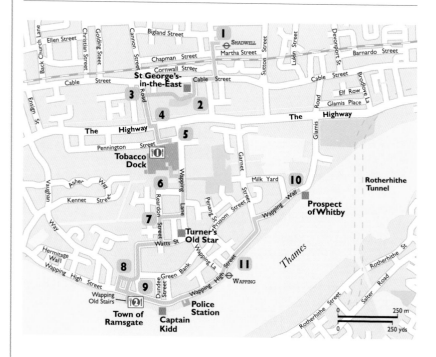

a lodger at the Pear Tree public house. A search of his belongings turned up a bloodstained knife, and the crimes had, as far as most people were concerned, been solved. He subsequently committed suicide in prison and his body was then paraded around Wapping before being buried at the crossroads to your right.

4 Turn left on to Cannon Street Road and go right at the traffic lights to cross the Highway by the traffic lights. As you do so, look at Machine Mart to your

right, on the approximate site of Timothy Marr's drapers shop. Veer left off the crossing and go right down Chigwell Hill. Turn left along Pennington Street then turn right into Tobacco Dock.

Tobacco Dock was built between 1811 and 1813 and was used for the storage of skins, tobacco, tea and spices. When the dock closed it was converted into a shopping centre but this enterprise failed and the place is now echoing, cavernous and largely empty.

WHERE TO EAT

🍴 **FRANK STEIN,**
Tobacco Dock;
Tel: 020 7488 2465.
Popular with locals, this is very much an East End 'caff'. Sandwiches, rolls and fry-ups are the order of the day.

🍴 **THE TOWN OF RAMSGATE,**
62 Wapping High Street;
Tel: 020 7481 8000.
Enjoy a hearty meal and a pint on the riverside balcony.

5 Go down the steps and pause by the statues of the tiger and little boy to the right. These commemorate the days when wild animals were landed at the docks and sold in nearby shops.

One day a tiger escaped from its crate at nearby Jamrach's Emporium and a little boy attempted to pat its nose. The animal picked him up in its jaws. Mr Jamrach raced from his shop, forced the tiger's jaws open and freed the unharmed boy. The full story of this event and of Jamrach's Emporium can be read on plaques to the left and right of the stairs.

6 Keep ahead through Tobacco Dock and be sure to admire the colourful collection of ships' figureheads as you leave. Pass along Porters Walk, which goes between two modern replicas of sailing ships, go up the steps and turn left. Walk up the next set of steps and turn right on to Wapping Lane. Take the

second right into Chandler Street, at the end of which go left along Reardon Street. Cross to its right.

On the wall on the right is a blue plaque marking the site of the house where Captain William Bligh, of mutiny on HMS *Bounty* fame, lived from 1785 to 1790. It was in Wapping that he took on Fletcher Christian, the man who led the famous mutiny against him.

7 Keep ahead along Reardon Street and go left on to Watts Street to pause alongside Turner's Old Star.

It is believed that the artist Joseph Turner (1775-1851) inherited this pub and gave it to his mistress Sophia Booth. A history of the pub is on a board outside.

8 Backtrack, then keep ahead along Watts Street, turn left into Tench Street, then go first right and turn left through the arched gate. Pass through the churchyard of St John's, a shady and sometimes sinister spot with tombstones lining its walls. The old charity school can be seen to the left beyond the railings. Although it has now been converted to flats, figures of a charity boy and girl can still be seen over its door. Exit the churchyard through the gate in the opposite right corner and go right into Wapping High Street. Take the first right into Pierhead, once the entrance to Wapping dock but long since filled in to provide a central garden for the surrounding houses – built in 1811 for dock officials. Walk anti-clockwise around this delightful square then go left along Wapping High Street. At the Town of Ramsgate pub, go right along the narrow passage to Wapping Old Stairs.

At low tide you can continue down the steps to the river bank. For more than 400 years, those convicted of piracy were hanged at Execution Dock, which stood to the left of the stairs. The bodies were left hanging until three tides had washed over them, after which they would be tarred and gibbeted as a warning to other seafarers tempted to seek booty from piracy. The most famous execution here was that of Captain William Kidd, who was hired to capture pirates on the high seas. He turned buccaneer himself and, on being caught, was convicted of murder and piracy. He was hanged on 23 May 1701 and a huge crowd turned out to watch him die. The rope broke on the first attempt, so the crowd enjoyed the added spectacle of watching him drop twice. His restless wraith is still said to wander the stairs when darkness falls.

9 Backtrack to the Town of Ramsgate, named for the fishermen from Ramsgate who once came to sell their fish at Wapping Old Stairs. Go right along Wapping High Street. Keep ahead past the Captain Kidd pub which occupies an old dock warehouse.

The curious white building is the River Police HQ. Thames River Police, founded in 1797 to combat the huge problem of theft from the docks, are the oldest uniformed force in the world.

10 Continue along Wapping High Street. Keep ahead past Wapping Station, go left into New Crane Place, right into Wapping High Street's continuation and keep walking to the Prospect of Whitby.

Built in 1520 and originally known as the Devil's Tavern because of the smugglers that made up its regular clientele, this is the oldest pub on the riverside. In 1777 it changed its name to honour a collier from Whitby named the *Prospect* that regularly moored alongside. Its interior is locked in a time warp and the pewter bar is propped up on beer barrels. The gallows on its riverside terrace remind you of its less salubrious past.

11 Backtrack towards Wapping Underground Station, where this walk ends. The station is closed until 2010 and a replacement bus service will take you back towards the City.

Wanderings and Wizards

This eventful walk begins alongside the Tower of London and twists its way through a fascinating warren of streets steeped in history.

On this walk you'll visit the principal site where public beheadings took place for more than 400 years and encounter a sinister-looking gate topped by stone skulls. The walk takes in the church where, after the ravages of the Great Fire of London, Samuel Pepys gazed down from the tower and witnessed a scene of utter desolation. It passes modern office blocks – behind which creepy passageways recall days gone by – and the gleaming modernity of the Lloyd's Insurance building. And, if all that isn't magical enough, you will also stroll through the beautiful Victorian market that is the location for Diagon Alley in the Harry Potter films. The final section of the walk takes you into a labyrinth of old alleyways through which you literally walk back in time. Here you will pass venerable old City eating houses, including the one where the infamous so-called Hellfire Club was founded, as you explore the alleyways where Charles Dickens began his most ghostly of tales, *A Christmas Carol*.

Christus mihi vere
Mors mihi lucrum
11mo April 1658

I Leave Tower Hill Underground Station and cross to Trinity Square Gardens. Veer left and follow the path as it swings right to pass the Mercantile Marine Memorial, paying homage to the 24,000 men of the Merchant Navy and Fishing Fleet who, during World War II, 'gave their lives for their country and have no grave but the sea'. Go up the three steps. On the right is the site of the ancient scaffold.

Between 1381 and 1747 more than 125 people were beheaded here. Sir Thomas More, Thomas Cromwell, Protector Somerset and the Earl of Monmouth are just a few of those who faced the immense crowds to whom these public spectacles proved an irresistible magnet. The last was the 80-year-old Jacobite, Lord Lovatt, executed here on 9 April 1747. He was astonished at the number of people who had come to watch him die. "God save us," he exclaimed, "why should there be such a bustle about taking off an old grey head?" Turning to the executioner he noticed that the man appeared nervous, and said, "Cheer up thy heart man, I am not afraid. Why should you be?" Kneeling, he placed his head on the block, commended his soul to God, and became the last person to be beheaded in England.

2 Turning your back on this memorial, leave the gardens via the gate to the right of the Mercantile Marine Memorial and cross the crossing, after which bear right to reach the church of All Hallows-by-the-Tower.

WHERE TO EAT

[O] THE HUNG, DRAWN AND QUARTERED,
27 Great Tower Street;
Tel: 020 7626 6123.
Functional as opposed to fashionable pub with a lovely interior. It can get crowded in the early evening.

[O] THE GEORGE AND VULTURE,
3 Castle Court;
Tel: 020 7626 9710.
Established in 1600 and a favourite of Charles Dickens, this tucked-away restaurant exists in a time warp. On the menu is traditional British fare such as devilled whitebait and steak and kidney pie.

Through its doors have stepped the likes of Bishop Lancelot Andrews and William Penn, both of whom were christened here in 1555 and 1644 respectively. The infamous Judge Jeffries was married at the church in 1667, as was John Quincy Adams – later sixth President of the United States – in 1797. After the Great Fire of London in 1666, Samuel Pepys climbed to the top of its tower and, gazing down upon the smouldering remains below, declared it 'the saddest sight of desolation'. The ghost of a Victorian choirmistress haunts the church, and in December 1920 she attended a choir rehearsal and listened to Christmas carols before disappearing.
ALL HALLOWS-BY-THE-TOWER;
www.allhallowsbythetower.org.uk

OPPOSITE: ST OLAVE'S CHURCH

DISTANCE 2 miles (3.2km)

ALLOW 1 hour 45 minutes

START Tower Hill Underground Station

FINISH Bank Underground Station

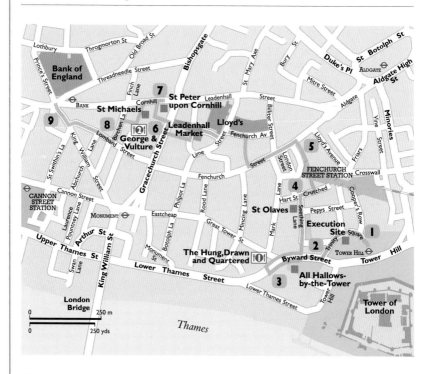

On the map: Lothbury, Throgmorton St, Old Broad St, Bishopsgate, St Mary Axe, Bury St, Duke's Pl, St Botolph St, Aldgate, Aldgate High St, Bank of England, Prince's Street, Threadneedle Street, Mitre Street, Finch Lane, Cornhill, BANK, St Michaels, **7** St Peter upon Cornhill, Leadenhall Street, Billiter Street, Minories, Vine Street, **9**, **8**, Birchin La, **6** George & Vulture, Leadenhall Market, Lloyd's, Fenchurch Av, Lime Street, Lloyd's Avenue, Friars, **5**, King William Street, St Swithin's La, Abchurch Lane, Gracechurch Street, Lombard Street, Philpot La, Rood Lane, Fenchurch, London Street, FENCHURCH STREET STATION, Crosswall, Cooper's Row, CANNON STREET STATION, Cannon Street, Laurence Pountney Lane, MONUMENT, Eastcheap, Great Tower St, Mincing Lane, Mark Lane, Hart St, **4**, Crutched Friars, St Olaves, Seething Lane, Pepys Street, Execution Site, Square, **1**, Upper Thames St, Arthur St, Swan Lane, King William St, Botolph La, Monument St, Lower Thames Street, The Hung, Drawn and Quartered, Byward Street, **2**, Trinity Square, TOWER HILL, Tower Hill, **3** All Hallows-by-the-Tower, London Bridge, Lower Thames Street, Tower of London, *Thames*

0 — 250 m
0 — 250 yds

3 Exit the church and go left along Byward Street. Cross the pedestrian crossing towards the Hung, Drawn and Quartered pub, named for the nearby executions. Cross Great Tower Street by the next crossing, swing right at the public toilets and take the first left into Seething Lane.

At the gardens on the right you'll see the bust of the diarist Samuel Pepys, which marks the site of the navy office where he began his career in 1660. At the end of Seething Lane on the left is the intriguing though decidedly gruesome-looking gateway of St Olave's, Hart Street. Dating from the late 17th century, this gateway decorated with skulls, crossbones and ferocious spikes was intended to act as a deterrent to the body snatchers who might be tempted to rob the graves of those buried in the churchyard.

ST OLAVE'S CHURCH;

DAILY 10-4 www.stolaveschurch.org.uk

4 Go right along Crutched Friars, which commemorates the House of the Friars of the Holy Cross that once stood here.

A brief history of it can be read on the wall of the Crutched Friar pub, a little way along on the left. They were known as the Crossed or Crux Friars, which over time became corrupted to the present name Crutched.

5 A little further along turn left into the dimly lit French Ordinary Court, which is little more than a dark tunnel that burrows through gloomy arches and has a sinister ambience. Turn left at its far side and walk through the narrow St Katharine's Row to emerge blinking into the daylight of Fenchurch Street where you turn left. Cross the crossing just past London Street and bear left then right into Fen Court. The chest tombs that you pass belonged to the now defunct churchyard of St Gabriel Fen Church. Go left along Fenchurch Avenue, left into Lime Street, turn right at the gleaming Lloyd's Building – with its glass elevators and shiny steel exterior – and keep ahead into the exquisite interior of Leadenhall Market.

Designed in 1881 by architect Horace Jones, Leadenhall Market is a place to wander at leisure and discover hidden shops, boutiques and delightful eateries. It recently became a star of the silver screen when it was used as the location for Diagon Alley in the film *Harry Potter and the Philosopher's Stone*. Beneath the clock and the three lights that mark its centre, turn left to take the second right into Bull's Head Passage to the building with the blue exterior. This was used as the entrance to the Leaky Cauldron pub in the same film.

6 At the end of Bull's Head Passage go right along Gracechurch Street, cross cautiously to its other side and just before Ede and Ravenscroft's clothing store go left into St Peter's Alley.

On the right is the church of St Peter upon Cornhill, reputedly the oldest Christian site in London dating back to AD 179, when it was founded by Lucius, the first Christian King of Britain. Follow the alley as it bears right then turn right along Cornhill to the front door of St Peter's. Look up at the building to its right and you'll see three terracotta demons grimacing back at you, their faces contorted with devilish hatred. In the 19th century the building from which they look down was designed by an architect named Rentz. Unfortunately, he inadvertently encroached onto church land and the vicar created such a fuss that Rentz was forced to revise his plans. The gremlins were his revenge and the face of the most ferocious one is said to be that of the vicar.

7 Backtrack along Cornhill. On arrival at the next church, St Michael's, go left through St Michael's Alley.

It was in this vicinity that Dickens set Scrooge's Counting House in

A Christmas Carol. Keep ahead through the dark passageway that passes the George and Vulture pub, which was established in 1600 and is the place where the first meeting of the Brotherhood of St Francis of Wycombe (universally known as Sir Francis Dashwood's Hellfire Club) allegedly took place in May 1746.

8 Go right through the even narrower Bengal Court and emerge at its far end to turn left along Birchen Lane.

On the wall to your left is an easily missed memorial to Captain Ralph Douglas Binney, a retired naval officer who in 1944 tried to thwart the getaway of Thomas Jenkins and Ronald Hedley, who had just robbed a jeweller's in Birchen Lane. As their car turned right into Lombard Street, Binney stepped out and tried to force them to stop. Instead they drove straight over him and dragged his body for more than a mile before dropping it on Tooley Street. In 1947 his Royal Navy colleagues instituted the Binney Memorial Medal, still awarded annually to the civilian the committee decides has performed the bravest action in support of law and order.

9 At the end of Birchen Lane go right along Lombard Street, noting the colourful signs hanging from the buildings' first-floor levels and keep ahead to Bank Underground Station.

Bards and Bawds in Southwark

Southwark is where many of Shakespeare's plays received their first airing, no doubt with the bard himself in attendance, or even performing.

The new Shakespeare's Globe that has risen on the banks of the Thames, close to the site of the original theatre, has brought a surge of visitors into an area that 20 years ago would have been right off the tourist map. Southwark is also the district where Charles Dickens's father, John, was imprisoned for debt, an event that so shocked 11-year-old Charles that his memory of it haunted him for the rest of his life. The walk visits the one surviving relic from the prison that both scarred the young Dickens emotionally yet also fired his imagination. It then hugs the riverside to view the site of the Clink, the prison that gave its name to all others; sees a wonderful fragment of a 14th-century bishops' palace; encounters a burial ground where paupers and prostitutes, 'the forgotten dead', were buried; and ends at an old operating theatre in a bizarre location – the roof space of a church. The opportunity to step inside the glorious interior of Southwark cathedral should most certainly not be passed up.

I Exit Borough station onto Borough High Street and go over to the church of St George the Martyr, which you can see opposite to the left. Turn right after the church into Tabard Street then turn left through the gates into St George's churchyard.

The dark brick wall opposite is all that remains of the Marshalsea Prison, which was closed in 1842. Charles Dickens's father, John, was imprisoned here for debt in 1824. A board to the right of the black gates provides a history.

2 Leave through the gates and turn left along Angel Place. On the wall on the left opposite the library you can look up at the large page facsimiles from Dickens's *Little Dorrit* showing original artworks from the book. Turn right along Borough High Street, go over the pedestrian crossing, off which bear left and go immediately right through Little Dorrit Court. On arrival at its far end go right along Redcross Street and turn left into Red Cross Garden.

This lovely garden, along with the hall and cottages that stand across from the gates, was laid out in 1887 by social reformer Mrs Octavia Hill on the site of a derelict paper factory. Her intention was to provide an open space for the poor who were crammed into the slums of the area. For six weeks she and her volunteers laboured to clear the site and burnt the remaining paper, which, given paper was then made from rags, meant the locals had to endure days of acrid smoke before

WHERE TO EAT

📍 **THE GEORGE INN,**
77 Borough High Street;
Tel: 020 7407 2056.
This is London's only surviving galleried coaching inn and is owned by the National Trust. Low beams, bundles of atmosphere and a menu that includes baps, sandwiches, salads and traditional English pies.

📍 **THE ANCHOR TAVERN,**
34 Park Street;
Tel: 020 7407 1577.
This cavernous 18th-century riverside pub is a Southwark institution. The older sections are incredibly atmospheric. All the pub favourites are here, from sausages and mash to roast beef, as well as baguettes and salads. Can get very crowded.

the garden was laid out. The wait must have been worth it though and, even today, this remains a tranquil oasis set amidst a sea of urban development.

3 Go left out of the garden and continue along Redcross Way. Keep ahead over Union Street and pause outside the gates on the right, to the right of which was the site of the Cross Bones Graveyard.

In medieval times this site was an unconsecrated graveyard for prostitutes who worked in the nearby brothels, most of which came under the jurisdiction

DISTANCE 3.5 miles (5.6km)

ALLOW 2 hours

START Borough Underground Station

FINISH London Bridge Station

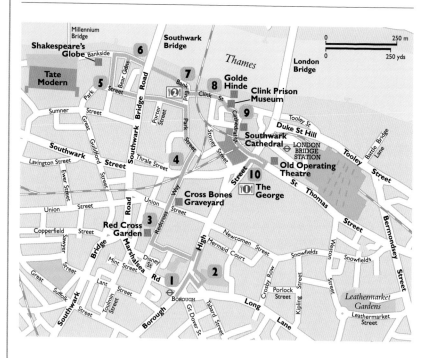

of the bishops of Winchester. By the 18th century it had become a paupers' burial ground, which closed in 1853. The graveyard was rediscovered when bodies were found during the building of the Jubilee Line. Since then local people have taken an interest in the forgotten graveyard and decorated the gates with ribbons, flowers and other objects to honour the 'outcast dead who were laid to rest here'. The area behind the gates, used as storage space by London Underground, contrasts sharply with

the brightly coloured commemorative ribbons that adorn the gates.

4 Keep ahead under the railway arch, and carefully cross Southwark Street to pass along the remainder of Red Cross Street. At the end turn left along Park Street. Go over Maiden Lane and follow Park Street to the left. Go over Porter Street and pause on the left.

Here is a plaque to Shakespeare's Globe Playhouse, which stood here from 1598

to 1613, when it burnt down during a performance of *Henry VIII*. A detailed history of the site can be read on the information boards behind it.

5 Continue along Park Street and go third right along New Globe Walk. At its end on the left is Shakespeare's Globe, the modern reproduction of the playhouse. A detour to visit its museum and exhibition is highly recommended. Go right along Bankside, passing Pizza Express, and go next right into Bear Gardens where immediately on the left is the Ferryman's Seat.

GLOBE EXHIBITION; OPEN DAILY
www.shakespeares-globe.org

Of uncertain age, but generally thought to be of 'ancient origins', the Ferryman's Seat once provided a convenient resting place for the Bankside watermen who ferried customers back and forth across the river from this spot.

6 Backtrack and continue right along Bankside. Veer right then left to pass under Southwark Bridge.

On the right are five granite panels on which are carved scenes from a frost fair on the Thames. These recall the days when the narrowness of old London Bridge slowed the flow of the river sufficiently for it to freeze over in cold winters. Londoners would move on to the ice to enjoy all manner of pastimes at frost fairs, the last of which took place in 1814. Read their history between each of the panels.

7 Continue along Bankside, turn right at the Anchor Tavern on to Bank End, then turn left into Clink Street. Directly ahead of you is the Clink Prison Museum.

The first prison was established here in 1127 and was a cellar in the Bishops of Winchester's Palace. All prisons on the site were known as the Clink and eventually 'to be in Clink' became synonymous with a spell in prison.

CLINK PRISON MUSEUM;
DAILY www.clink.co.uk

THE GOLDEN HINDE

8 Keep ahead along Clink Street, passing under the gibbet that swings menacingly above you. Keep ahead past Stoney Street and pause on the right alongside the remains of the Bishops of Winchester's Palace. A full history can be read on the information board. Continue ahead and go left on arrival at the replica of the *Golden Hinde*.

A wall plaque just past the ship narrates the legend of Mary Overie, whose father, John Overie, was a wealthy ferryman. He was also a notorious miser who one day he had the bright idea of feigning death in order that his servants might mourn his passing by fasting, thus saving him the cost of a day's food and drink. Unfortunately, his servants were so overjoyed when they learned of their master's death that they held a lavish party around his supposed corpse. John Overie listened to the sounds of merriment for as long as he could and then, seeking to admonish his ungrateful employees, he sat bolt upright with a roar of indignation. One of the servants thought that the devil was rising in the master's likeness, took up an oar, struck him over the head and killed him outright.

GOLDEN HINDE;
OPEN DAILY www.goldenhinde.org

9 Backtrack past the *Golden Hinde* and keep ahead into Cathedral Street, passing Southwark Cathedral on the left – you might like to make a detour to look at its colourful memorials to Shakespeare and John Gower, the father of English poetry.

Pass under the railway bridge, where the street name changes to Bedale Street. Go over Borough High Street at the traffic lights and keep ahead along the left side of St Thomas Street.

A little way along on the left go in through the doors of St Thomas's church tower, climb the narrow wooden staircase to the church's roof space, and marvel at a unique museum. This roof space was once the herb garret of St Thomas's hospital. From 1822 to 1862 it housed the hospital's female operating theatre. This was rediscovered in 1956, has since been restored and its displays give a vivid impression of surgical science in the days before either anaesthetic or basic hygiene were high on the list of a surgeon's priorities. It was at St Thomas's that Florence Nightingale founded her School of Nursing and a photograph once taken inside the museum showed a ghostly image that some claimed may well have been Florence Nightingale herself.

THE OLD OPERATING THEATRE;
OPEN DAILY 10.30-5
www.thegarret.org.uk

SOUTHWARK CATHEDRAL;
DAILY SERVICES IN THE CATHEDRAL
www.southwark.anglican.org/cathedral

10 Leave the church tower and go right along St Thomas Street. Turn left at the traffic lights. Along on the left is London Bridge Station, but before leaving the area, pass the station and turn left into the courtyard of the George Inn (1677), London's only surviving galleried coaching inn.

Shipshape in Greenwich

Greenwich is best known for its maritime history and as the location of Greenwich Mean Time, but it has a lot more to offer the casual stroller.

This walk begins with the opportunity to visit the majestic church of St Alfege, designed by Nicholas Hawksmoor and a spectacular statement in architecture. There follows an uphill trudge that ends at the Ranger's House where, in addition to exploring its magnificent rooms, you can marvel at one of the world's most remarkable collections of jewellery and Old Masters. From here the walk moves to the Royal Observatory, the origins of which go back to the reign of Charles II. A downhill walk through Greenwich Park brings you to the Queen's House, which as well as being a delightful building has several ghostly tales to chill the marrow. From here you enter the grounds of the Old Royal Naval College to gaze upon one of the most exquisitely painted dining halls in the western world. The walk ends alongside the *Cutty Sark*, the most famous sailing ship in the world. At the time of writing, the devastating fire of 2007 has plunged the future of this riverside treasure into uncertainty. Hopefully, its dedicated band of restorers will ensure that it is returned to its former glory.

Turn left out of Cutty Sark station and go right along Greenwich Church Street. Keep ahead over the traffic lights, and a little way along the street turn right through the gates of St Alfege church.

Alfege became the 29th Archbishop of Canterbury in 1006 at a time when the Kent coast was being subjected to raids from Danish pirates. In 1011 they laid siege to the city of Canterbury, took Alfege captive and brought him to Greenwich. He was held for six months and the Danes demanded a ransom of £3,000, which Alfege refused to allow his people to pay. At a feast on Easter Day his captors began bludgeoning him with ox bones and the shafts of their axes, until one of the Danes took pity on his plight and ended his suffering with a single axe blow to his head. A church was built on the site of St Alfege's martyrdom and the present building was built between 1712 and 1714 to a design by Nicholas Hawksmoor. The immense interior is breathtaking in its proportions and the central space was, at the time of its construction, the largest unsupported ceiling in Europe.

SAT-SUN 12-4 www.st-alfege.org

2 Walk anti-clockwise all the way around the exterior of the church and exit left from the gates along Greenwich Church Street. Cross the traffic lights to the right, off which bear right and keep ahead along the opposite side of Greenwich Church Street. Veer left along Stockwell Street, keep ahead

WHERE TO EAT

⦿ THE TRAFALGAR TAVERN,
6 Park Row;
Tel: 020 8858 2909.
This magnificent riverside pub was built in 1837, and was once famous for its whitebait suppers attended by senior Members of Parliament. Although not as popular a dish as it once was, the pub still serves whitebait, as well as a good selection of other traditional English meals.

⦿ THE PAVILION TEA HOUSE,
Greenwich Park;
Tel: 020 8858 9695.
This busy restaurant offers wholesome soups and a variety of meals that include shepherd's pie, Welsh rarebit, plus a range of salads and sandwiches.

over Nevada Street on to Croom's Hill and head up its right side, passing the Fan Museum which occupies two elegant Georgian buildings and boasts the largest collection of fans in the world. Continue up Croom's Hill and cross to its left side once over King George Street. Go over Park Walk and along the red gravel path to pause outside The Ranger's House.

Built in 1723, this stylish Georgian villa became the official residence of the Ranger of Greenwich Park in the 19th century. Today it houses the Wernher Collection – more than 650 exhibits put

DISTANCE **4 miles (6.4km)**

ALLOW **2 hours**

START **Docklands Light Railway Cutty Sark Station**

FINISH **Docklands Light Railway Cutty Sark Station**

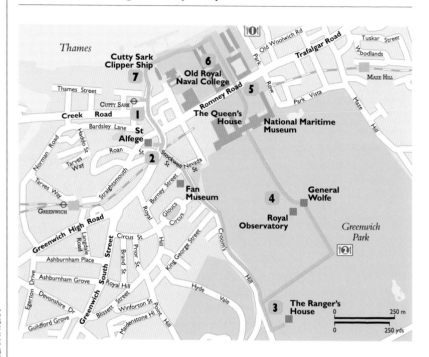

together around 1900 by the diamond magnate Sir Julius Wernher. Treasures on display include rare Old Masters and exquisite jewellery, including an opal-encrusted gold lizard pendant adorned with rubies for its collar and tongue.

RANGER'S HOUSE;

APR-SEP SUN-WED 10-5

www.english-heritage.org.uk/rangershouse

FAN MUSEUM;

TUE-SAT 11-5, SUN 12-5

www.fan-museum.org

3 Exit Ranger's House and retrace your footsteps, turning right along Park Walk. Follow it left and enter Greenwich Park through the gate on the right. Keep ahead along the path that runs between the litter and dog-waste bins. Go over the road and follow the path past the tree on its other side. Turn left and proceed past the buildings of the Royal Observatory, and bear right towards the statue of James Wolfe (1727-1759) and pause in front of it.

From this viewpoint you look down across Docklands – a silver plaque helps pinpoint which buildings are which. Walk to the left, where you will find the entrance to the Royal Observatory, founded by Charles II for the study of astronomy and longitude. The red Time Ball was installed on the roof of the Observatory in 1833 and was the first public time signal. The ball drops every day at exactly 1pm and since it can be clearly seen from the river, ships once used it to check their time. Loved by tourists, it is a curious sight to watch.

OBSERVATORY; DAILY 10-5

www.rog.nmm.ac.uk.

4 With your back to the Observatory entrance, bear diagonally left and go through the black gates where brass strips on the ground and walls mark the exact site of the line of the meridian. It is possible to straddle the line with a foot in each hemisphere. Exit the gates and go left down the steps. Descend the steep path and, at its end, veer right and take the second right path. At the foot of that, keep ahead through the gates towards the statue of Captain James Cook, in front of which go right to pass the buildings of the National Maritime Museum. Go first left, following the sign for Queen's House. Go right along the covered passage, and just before the next steps, go left down the steps and walk round to the entrance of the Queen's House.

The Queen's House was commissioned by Anne of Denmark, wife of James I.

James reputedly gave her the manor of Greenwich to apologize for swearing at her in public after she accidentally shot one of his favourite dogs while out hunting in 1614. She commissioned Inigo Jones to design the house, but construction was halted when she died in 1719. Ten years later, Charles I gave it to his new queen, Henrietta Maria. Inigo Jones was recalled and the exterior work was completed. The queen's tenure ended with the Civil War, although her son Charles II enlarged it upon his restoration and Queen Henrietta returned and remained in residence until her death in 1669. The Royal Hospital School was located here from 1821 to 1933. Many pupils told tales of ghosts haunting the tunnels under the Queen's House. One was of a maid who fell to her death over the handrail of the Tulip Staircase and whose ghost can be seen trying to clean the blood stain from the floor.

QUEEN'S HOUSE; DAILY 10-5

www.nmm.ac.uk

5 Leave the Queen's House. If you want to, you can make a diversion to visit the National Maritime Museum but otherwise keep ahead out of the gates, carefully cross Romney Road, and pass through the Royal Gate to enter The Royal Naval College.

The college was established by Royal Charter in 1694 as a hospital for retired seamen. The number of pensioners declined in the 19th century and it closed in 1869. Thereafter it became the Royal Naval College, a training centre for naval officers from around the world. The buildings are now occupied by Greenwich University. Keep ahead along the central path and at its end, just before the steps, go left and enter the Painted Hall, probably the finest dining hall in the western world. The spectacular paintings that adorn it were created by James Thornhill and took 19 years to complete, during which time the Greenwich Pensioners could not eat in what was intended to be their dining hall. Once completed (in 1727) it became such a tourist attraction that the pensioners still couldn't use it! The Queen Anne Building of the complex is haunted by the ghost of Admiral Byng, who was accused of cowardice for failing to 'do his utmost' during the Battle of Minorca in 1756. He was executed by firing squad on 14 March 1757. He still roams the rooms where he was confined at the college.

MUSEUM; DAILY 10-5 www.nmm.ac.uk
COLLEGE; DAILY 10-5
www.oldroyalnavalcollege.org

6 Exit the Painted Hall. If you want to, cross to the other side of the courtyard and visit the chapel. Otherwise go left down the steps and ahead along the central paved path to pass the statue of George II. This is the site of Greenwich Palace, birthplace of Henry VIII in 1491 and of his daughters Mary I and Elizabeth I in 1516 and 1533 respectively. Go out through the Watergate and turn left along the riverside until you arrive at Greenwich Pier; the Cutty Sark is to the left.

Built in 1869 at the height of British imperial grandeur, the Cutty Sark plied the high seas between Britain and China throughout the 1870s. She would go out carrying alcohol, and come back loaded with more than 1,400 tons of tea. The ship acquired a new lease of life in the 1880s with record-breaking trips transporting wool from Australia to England. Since 1954 she has been dry docked in Greenwich and more than 15 million visitors have stepped aboard. But tragedy beset the old vessel when at 4.45am on 21 May 2007 a fire broke out and ripped through the timbered ship. Fortunately, much of the structure was in storage and not affected. There are firm plans to restore her to her former glory.
www.cuttysark.org.uk

7 Go left past the Cutty Sark, keep going past the Gypsy Moth Pub and, just after Waterstones, go right to arrive back at Cutty Sark station, where this walk ends.

CUTTY SARK

Hauntings of Barnes Common

Overgrown cemeteries, a shrine to a rock legend and tales of a fire-breathing monster enliven a walk across Barnes Common.

In 1837 tales began of a strange fire-breathing creature haunting the wilder reaches of Barnes Common. It became known as Spring Heeled Jack and soon sightings were being reported across the country. Who or what he was has never been ascertained, but trek across Barnes Common and you can see why he chose to make his first leap into legend in this wild and mysterious place. But before you encounter Jack you will come across two more legends, one of 1970s glam rock music and one of crime. The walk begins with a visit to the spot where Marc Bolan died in 1977: a roadside shrine to his memory makes a poignant first stop. From here you venture into the wild hinterland of the common to learn of the exploits of famous highwayman Dick Turpin. By way of a creepy and overgrown cemetery, you will take a stroll along the banks of the River Thames and enter a secluded churchyard where one of the most eccentric tombs in the country looms over you. By climbing a ladder you can actually gaze in on the coffins of a famed Victorian explorer and his wife, a strange end to a walk that abounds with peculiar sights – and sites.

1 Leave Barnes Station via the exit on platform 4 and turn left through the concrete bollards across from the steps. Go along the asphalt path and at its end turn left along Queen's Ride. Cross cautiously to its right side and follow the earth path that runs alongside the brown brick wall. A little way along on the left, pause by the memorial to rock legend Marc Bolan (1947-77).

At around 5am on 16 September 1977 Marc was being driven home by his American girlfriend Gloria Jones when she lost control of the car on this bend and smashed into a tree. Bolan died instantly after his side of the car took the full impact of the crash. He was 29 years old – just two weeks short of his 30th birthday. The bronze bust at the top of the steps that lead up to the tree was unveiled on the 25th anniversary of the accident by Marc's son Rolan.

2 Go back down the steps, turn left then go left up the steps opposite the gate of No. 9. Cross Gypsy Lane, bear left then right along Queen's Ride, and ahead over the railway bridge. On its other side, cross over the road and go down the steps to bear right on to the earth path that passes under a tree. Keep ahead on to the football pitch. Go right at the goal posts and, once past the bench, keep ahead on to the grass path. Keep going over the asphalt path to pass beneath the low-hanging spreading branches of a tree and follow that path as it bends left, then right, and twists through some much thicker woodland.

WHERE TO EAT

[O] OLD SORTING OFFICE COMMUNITY ARTS CENTRE CAFÉ, Barnes Pond, 19-21 Station Road; Tel: 020 8876 9885. www.osoarts.org.uk
Offering all-day breakfasts and filling lunches, this place is alongside Barnes Pond and makes a nice venue to catch your breath after your trek across the common.

[O] YE WHITE HART, The Terrace, Riverside; Tel: 020 8876 5177.
A huge pub dating from 1662, although it was rebuilt in the early 20th century, giving it an Edwardian air. Delightful riverside balconies on which to enjoy a meal (traditional pub grub, slightly pricey), and a great place to watch the annual boat race.

You are now wandering the less frequented reaches of Barnes Common which, in the 1730s, were a favoured haunt of that most legendary of highwaymen, Dick Turpin. The thick foliage provided the perfect cover from which he and his accomplice Thomas Rowden could ride out and rob travellers as they crossed the common, which was then much wilder than it is today.

3 On emerging into a clearing take the path to the right and keep ahead over Common Road. Pick up the path again on its other side and follow it

149

DISTANCE **5.5 miles (8.8km)**

ALLOW **2 hours 45 minutes**

START **Barnes Station**

FINISH **Barnes Bridge Station**

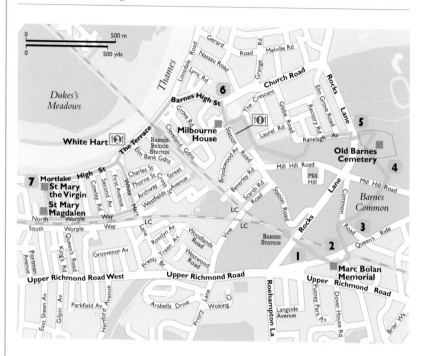

as it bends left then twists through bracken and gorse. When you reach its convergence with four other paths, take the one that bends sharp left and follow it as it bears left and passes a bench through a tunnel of trees, after which cross over Mill Hill Road and pick up the path again by the metal drain cover.

It was in this vicinity that sightings of Spring Heeled Jack, one of the 19th century's most elusive figures, were first reported. One night in September 1837

a businessman, crossing the common on his way home, was suddenly startled by a hideous-looking figure that vaulted over some railings and landed with a thud in front of him. One look at its pointed ears, glowing eyes, and prominent nose was sufficient to send the man fleeing in terror. Over the next few months a ghost, imp or devil carried out a number of attacks on people as they crossed the common at night. From these beginnings Spring Heeled Jack, or at least his legend, captured the Victorian

public's imagination and sightings of him were reported all over the country for many years afterwards. The mystery of who, or what, the monster was has never been solved, although the finger of suspicion has been pointed at a Marquis of Waterford who apparently enjoyed jumping out on people and pinning them to the ground in lonely country lanes.

4 On arrival at the bench, go left along the asphalt path and just before the car park turn right to enter the Old Cemetery, which is one of the eeriest and seemingly neglected burial grounds imaginable.

Toppled monuments litter overgrown paths, an abundance of headless stone angels struggle to free themselves from clinging greenery. It is little wonder that tales of ghostly figures, including a floating nun who hovers over the cemetery, are whispered of in hushed tones by those who pass through this creepy, yet truly atmospheric place.

5 When the path divides, take the left fork and follow that as it bears right to keep ahead past the large memorial to William Hedgeman. On arrival at the red marble lozenge grave of Claude Henry Leach, bear left along that path and on the right at the end is the gravestone of the artist Alexander Joseph Finberg (1866-1897). Keep ahead past the tree towards the tennis courts, step down off the wall and go left along the path. As the fence ends, go right along the asphalt path and prepare to be

jolted back to the 21st century as you turn right on to the very busy Rocks Lane. Cross over the pedestrian crossing, off which bear right and go first left into Ranelagh Avenue. Opposite its junction with Bellevue Road, go left along the asphalt path and after a slight ascent turn right then right again just after the bench.

At the end of that path, as you arrive before the line of houses, there is a Barnes Common Nature Reserve Information Board with interesting information. Go right in front of the houses and pass over the little footbridge beneath which flows the Beverley Brook, so called because beavers once lived on its waters. On the other side of the bridge take the left fork and keep ahead to pass Barnes Pond. Cross over Station Road, bear left and a little way along on the right is Milbourne House, the oldest building in Barnes, parts of which date from the 1400s. Well hidden behind the creepers on the wall is a blue plaque to Henry Fielding who bought the house in 1748, the year before he enjoyed success with his novel *Tom Jones*.

6 Backtrack and keep ahead past Essex Lodge. Go left along Barnes High Street at the end of which go left on to The Terrace, where a picturesque reach of the River Thames lies beyond the right side. Pass under the railway bridge of Barnes Bridge Station and opposite the White Hart Pub go left along White Hart Lane. Just before the railway crossing, go right along North

Worple Way. Just after passing Worple Street, go right and cross to the easily missed Church of St Mary Magdalen.

Enter the churchyard through the door to its left, go clockwise around the church and cross to the far wall to the tomb of Victorian explorer and linguist, Sir Richard Burton (1821-1890). Burton is buried in a stone replica of a Bedouin tent that stands 12ft (3.7m) square by 18ft (5.5m) high and is adorned with a frieze of Islamic crescents and stars. Startling as this incongruous monument is, yet another surprise awaits you if you make your way to the rear of the tomb and climb the ladder to peer through the glass plate at the interior. You are looking down upon the coffins of Burton and his wife, surrounded by dusty artefacts such as lamps and helmets.

7 Backtrack along North Worple Way and take the first left along Worple Street. At its end, turn left along the paved alley, turn right and, just before reaching the church of St Mary the Virgin, go right through the gate and walk into the churchyard. Having passed through the stone arch, read the history board and learn about those who are buried here.

Backtrack out of the gate and go right. If the church is open it is well worth a visit. Go right along Mortlake High Street where you can catch buses to Richmond – cross the street for buses to Barnes and Hammersmith. Or keep ahead into The Terrace, go past the White Hart and a little further along on the right you come to Barnes Bridge Station, from which trains depart for Central London.

Murder in Richmond

This is a long walk, part of which takes you across the picturesque reaches of Richmond Park, with tales of murder and aristocratic ghosts.

The walk begins by exploring the few remaining fragments of Richmond Palace, where both Henry VII and Elizabeth I died. From here you will descend towards the river for a stroll along the Thames, before an uphill climb to a viewpoint where a stunning vista unfolds before you. Via the site of a particularly gruesome murder, and through a creepy passageway that squeezes between two halves of a cemetery, you will pass into Richmond Park. Here you can enjoy a decidedly rural stroll to a mound from which legend – though not history – maintains that Henry VIII watched for a signal from the Tower of London that Anne Boleyn was dead. The final section of the walk takes you along a beautiful stretch of the Thames to Ham House, a grand old property where ghostly tales abound. Be sure to time your walk to allow plenty of time to visit the house. As a whole, this walk comprises an eclectic mix of country rambling and historical places and, as such, will provide both a memorable and fascinating outing.

1 Exit Richmond Station and go left along The Quadrant. Go over the zebra crossing, off which bear left and go right at the traffic lights along Duke Street to arrive at Little Green. Cross diagonally left towards the Green, which began as a common on which villagers pastured their sheep but later became a medieval jousting ground for Richmond Palace. Pause to read the information board that provides a little more history then take the left path to the left of the board (a black-on-yellow arrow points the way). On the other side of the Green turn right at the tiny hut. Cross to the opposite side and keep ahead, passing on your left Maids of Honour Row, a row of sedate Georgian houses built by the Prince of Wales, later George II, for the ladies-in-waiting to the Princess of Wales, Caroline of Anspach. Go next left and pause before the gatehouse of Richmond Palace.

You'll find a full history of the palace behind the red mail box on the opposite side of the road from where you turned. The Tudor palace was built by Henry VII, whose coat of arms can be seen on the gatehouse as you approach. Only this and parts of the old wardrobe beyond now survive from that building. Henry VII died here, and his son, Henry VIII, lived here, until Cardinal Wolsey 'gave' him Hampton Court Palace. Elizabeth I also died at the palace. As the old queen lay dying, at 10pm on 23 March 1603, one of her ladies-in-waiting left the room and was walking along a gloomy corridor when she spied Elizabeth's unmistakable figure striding towards her. Thinking the queen had made a recovery she raced back to the royal bedchamber but found her mistress breathing her last. Perhaps Elizabeth's spirit had taken one last stroll around the palace? During the Civil War of 1642-51 Oliver Cromwell demolished the most important buildings, leaving these few remnants to hint at what a magnificent structure it must have been.

2 Pass through the gatehouse into Old Palace Yard and keep ahead, passing the Wardrobe on your left. Turn right in front of Trumpeter's House to forge ahead along the path beyond the two white bollards with the EIIR crest on them. Turn left and head down to the river and, as the path veers left by Asgill House, you will find a board giving a full history of the Old Deer Park. Go left by the board and keep ahead to pass under the bridge and turn immediately left up the steps into O'Higgin's Square. Turn left, go up the steps and bear right towards the Odeon Cinema, and go right on to Hill Rise. Go over the pedestrian crossing, off which bear right and keep ahead up Richmond Hill. Cross to its right side and keep going until, having passed Friars Stile Road on the left, you are opposite Norfolk Lodge.

Pause here and take in one of the most awe-inspiring vistas imaginable. There is an information board to help you pinpoint the sights that unfold before you. This is the only view in England to be protected by an Act of Parliament – it was passed in 1902 to preserve the view

DISTANCE **5 miles (8km)**

ALLOW **3 hours**

START **Richmond Station**

FINISH **Richmond Station**

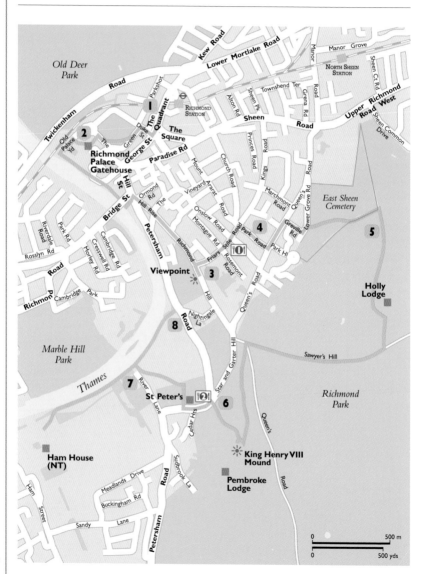

that has been acclaimed by artists such as Turner and Reynolds and writers such as Sir Walter Scott, who described it as 'an unrivalled landscape'.

3 Backtrack and go right along Friars Stile Road. Take the fourth right along Park Road and pause a little way along on the right, outside No. 9.

In February 1879, this house was known as 2 Vine Cottages and was owned by Mrs Julia Thomas, a fastidious woman whose servant, Kate Webster, failed to satisfy her employer's exacting demands for tidiness and was duly dismissed. On Sunday 2 March, her last day in service, Kate – who had spent the day drinking in the Hole in the Wall pub (which still stands a few doors along) – murdered Mrs Thomas by throwing her down the stairs. She then cut up the body, boiled down the flesh and disposed of it all in the Thames. Kate was arrested and executed for the crime, gruesome evidence of which was provided by the landlady of the Hole in the Wall who told how, the day after the murder, Kate had tried to sell her two jars of fat!

4 Continue along Park Road and go left along Queen's Road. Cross it via the crossing a little past Queen's Rise, off which veer right and go left into Greville Road. At the end turn left on to Lower Grove Road. Take the first right and veer left along the earth path that squeezes between the hedges and fences of East Sheen Cemetery. Follow the path through the woodland and when you

arrive at a shin-high wooden barrier go right and pass through the gate into Richmond Park.

Unlike the Old Deer Park, which is deer-less, 300 red and 350 fallow deer roam free in this beautiful park. In recent years they have been joined by a phantom cavalier who, according to reports in the local press, has been sighted roaming through the foliage.

5 Continue ahead on to the main red gravel path to the right of the Nature Reserve information board, passing on your left the fenced-off enclosure of Holly Lodge. A little way past the lodge the path forks, but keep straight, heading for the road in the distance and turn right along it. Go left at the roundabout along Queen's Road. Cross to the right side and follow the far right path that runs alongside the iron fence. Go through the gate to the right of Pembroke Lodge (the small building with the single chimney), and keep ahead into Pembroke Lodge Gardens. Pass through the beautiful John Beer Laburnum Walk, and fork left directly after it, where you'll see an information board about King Henry VIII's mound. Take the middle of the three paths to the left and follow it to the top of the mound where you can admire another stunning view.

The mound is reputedly named for the fact that Henry VIII stood on top of it on 19 May 1536 to watch for the rocket fired from the Tower of London to signal that Anne Boleyn was dead and he was free to marry Jane Seymour. The views from the summit are truly stunning and it is possible to see Windsor Castle and St Paul's Cathedral.

6 Backtrack towards the John Beer Laburnum Walk and veer sharp left in front of it. Go down the hill and, just as you arrive at the open green on your left, bear right along the rough earth path and pass through the gate on the right. Follow the downhill path as it goes right towards the children's playground in the distance. Bear right along the red gravel path, pass through the gate and turn left along Petersham Road. Cross to its right side and take the narrow right turn signed Petersham Nurseries.

You will pass the small and picturesque St Peter's church. West Coast Canadians might like to go into the churchyard to view the grave of George Vancouver, who discovered Vancouver Island.

7 When you arrive at the iron gate, keep ahead along the asphalt path (a black-on-yellow arrow points the direction). Go through the swing gate and keep straight to pass through the next gate. Turn left to follow the beautiful, though often muddy, riverside path for three quarters of a mile until you veer left through the trees and arrive at Ham House.

Known as the Sleeping Beauty of country houses, this splendid building dates from 1610 and is reputedly one

WHERE TO EAT

[**IOI**] **THE MARLBOROUGH,**
46 Friars Stile Road;
Tel: 020 8940 0572.
Having struggled up Richmond Hill and before you venture out into the wilds of Richmond Park, take a break in this airy and pleasant bar.

[**IOI**] **THE DYSART,**
135 Petersham Road;
Tel: 020 8940 8005.
Once you have trekked across the park to Petersham Road, on the right is this welcoming black-and-white timber-fronted pub. Good food and a lovely beer garden.

of the most haunted houses in England, with as many as 15 ghosts, especially that of the ruthlessly ambitious Elizabeth Murray, Lady Dysart. Some members of staff are so convinced of her presence that they enter the room with a respectful "Good day, your Ladyship." Guides report being shoved in the back by an unseen hand on the stairs, footprints have appeared overnight on floors, and a ghostly spaniel-like dog has been seen trotting along corridors.

8 Backtrack along the river path. When you arrive at the gate where you joined the path, bear left and on arrival at the white building veer right on to Petersham Road. You can catch a 65 bus back to Richmond Station, or walk it in 15 minutes by keeping ahead.

RICHMOND PARK

The Chilling Streets
of Chiswick

Chiswick has one of London's loveliest riversides, where grand old houses testify that this neighbourhood was once far removed from the city.

Just a stone's throw away, Chiswick's idyllic riverside setting gives way to the traffic on the Great West Road, hurtling in and out of London, most of the drivers oblivious to the almost pastoral scene that lies close by. This walk reflects the contrasts of the area. It begins by crossing a delightful square that would be more at home in Brighton or Cheltenham and yet finds itself marooned between two very busy main roads. It drifts into the tranquillity of the riverside, to visit a lovely old pub where a decidedly sinister event occurred 200 years ago. Then, just as you are absorbing the ambience of the beautiful Chiswick Mall, who should make an unexpected appearance but one of the leading contenders for the mantle of Jack the Ripper? Having enjoyed an eventful and varied stroll, the walk gets even more charming towards its end as you have the opportunity to visit two wonderful old properties, Chiswick House and Hogarth's House – be sure to plan your walk to ensure you can fit them both in.

1. Leave Stamford Brook station and go right along Goldhawk Road. At the traffic lights, turn left on to King Street and go immediately right into St Peter's Square. Keep ahead, passing to the right of its central garden. The square dates from the 1830s and many of its gleaming white three-storey houses have decorative eagles and lions outside. The properties look a little out of place here, as though they'd be more at home in a provincial setting. Go left after the gardens and keep ahead towards St Peter's, Hammersmith. Just before the church, go right through the iron arch then right again to pass through the subway out of which go right along South Black Lion Lane. Near the end on the left is the Black Lion Pub.

Towards the end of 1803 a spectral white figure began terrifying late-night wanderers in the vicinity of Black Lion Lane. One night just before Christmas the 'ghost' attacked a local woman who had taken a short cut home through the churchyard. So great was her shock that she took to her bed and died shortly afterwards. On the night of 3 January 1804 a young Excise man named Francis Smith 'filled his blunderbuss with shot and himself with ale' and lay in wait for the ghost on Black Lion Lane. Just before 11pm a white figure came strolling towards him and Smith shot at it. To his horror he discovered that he had killed a white-clothed plasterer named Thomas Millwood, who was simply on his way home. The body was brought to the Black Lion and the inquest was held

there. The story is told on an information board on the pub's outer wall.

2. Turn left out of the pub and go right along Hammersmith Terrace, keeping ahead until the road becomes Chiswick Mall. Once you've passed Miller's Court on the right pause a few doors along outside the gabled cream house named Osiers, built about 1786.

In 1888 the house was owned by Harry Wilson, a member of the Cambridge Conversazione Society, widely known as The Apostles. Many of the members were prominent though secretive homosexuals, and Wilson's house acted as a 'chummery' at which fellow Apostles were welcome day or night. Montague John Druitt, a major Jack the Ripper suspect, may have visited the house on occasion. Since his body was found floating in the stretch of the river near the house, it has been suggested that Druitt may have sought Wilson's assistance and, on being turned away, committed suicide by throwing himself into the Thames.

3. Keep walking along Chiswick Mall and pause on the right outside Walpole House, a magnificent 16th-century house that was altered in the 17th and 18th centuries.

It was reputedly the home of one of Charles II's most famous mistresses, Barbara Villiers, Duchess of Cleveland, for the last two years of her life. Although once famed for her beauty, by the time she arrived in Chiswick her weight had

DISTANCE 4 miles (6.4km)

ALLOW 2 hours 30 minutes

START Stamford Brook Underground Station

FINISH Burlington Lane bus stops

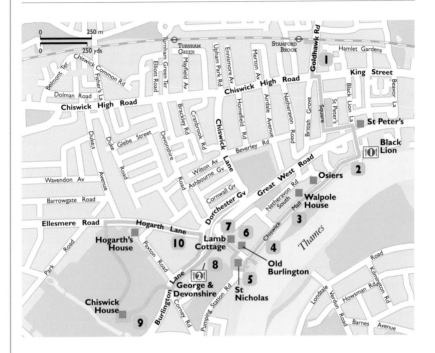

ballooned and her looks had faded. Local residents whispered of seeing her standing at a window in the moonlight begging for her beauty to be restored. Following her death in 1709, her ghost reputedly continued with these late-night vigils.

4 Stroll along Chiswick Mall, pausing outside Red Lion House built about 1700 and for many years the Red Lion pub. It was also the childhood home of Sir Peter Saunders, the theatrical impresario who first staged Agatha Christie's *The Mousetrap*. Just before the road forks right towards the church, go left on to Church Street Causeway and pause on the banks of the river.

A history of the Causeway can be read on the wall to the right. It was hereabouts that the body of Montague John Druitt was found floating in the Thames on 30 December 1888.

5 Backtrack and keep ahead on to Church Street to go left through

the gate and up the steps into the churchyard of St Nicholas's church.

A little way in on the left is the railed tomb of artist William Hogarth, who lies buried with his wife and mother-in-law. The grave's epitaph was composed by the actor David Garrick. Go through the church porch and bear right through the gate to proceed clockwise around the church. Although the body of the church was rebuilt in 1882, the tower mostly dates from 1446 and is the oldest part of the building. Oliver Cromwell's daughters, Mary Fauconberg and Frances Rich, are buried in the church, albeit their vault has no memorial. It is also possible that Oliver Cromwell himself lies in the same place. During the 1882 rebuilding the vault was opened and a battered coffin, not mentioned in the register, was sighted. But since Cromwell's name was unpopular at the time, the possible discovery was not publicized and the vault was bricked up and left unmarked. However, you might catch a glimpse of Mary's and Frances's ghosts which are said to haunt the churchyard.

6 Keep ahead to the black-and-white timbered house, the Old Burlington, a beautiful Elizabethan building that was once a pub called the Burlington Arms.

Dick Turpin is said to have held his marriage breakfast at the hostelry and on one occasion the forces of law and order spotted his horse tied up outside and hammered on the door calling for him to come out. Turpin raced upstairs, leapt from an upstairs window on to his horse, and galloped away. The building became a private house in 1924.

7 Go left in front of the Old Burlington and pause outside the attractive pink-and-white Lamb Cottage. This was formerly the Lamb Tap pub and it was here that the inquest into the death of Montague John Druitt was held.

His brother William Druitt, a solicitor, testified that Montague, who was 31, had been a barrister-at-law, and an assistant master at a school in Blackheath. On 11 December 1888, William heard that his brother had not been seen at his barrister's chambers for over a week and so he went to the school to make enquiries about him. He was told that Montague had got into serious trouble and had been dismissed. On searching his belongings William found what appeared to be a suicide note which ended 'the best thing for me was to die'. A verdict of suicide was returned.

8 Keep ahead along Church Street and go left on to Burlington Lane. Immediately after the George and Devonshire pub go left into Chiswick Square, possibly the smallest square in London, with houses that date from around 1680. Backtrack and go left along Burlington Lane and cross it at the pedestrian crossing, off which bear left and go right through the small stone gate into the grounds of Chiswick House. Turn left and just past the 5mph speed limit sign, go right along the earth path through the trees and follow it to the large gateposts of the house.

A magnificent example of Palladian architecture, Chiswick House was built between 1725 and 1729 for Richard Boyle, 3rd Earl of Burlington. It was intended as a monument to his appreciation of art. In the 19th century it became a lunatic asylum, but by the mid 20th century it had fallen into ruin. Now the responsibility of English Heritage, the house has been beautifully restored. Several visitors have sensed a female presence in the bedchamber and one woman even saw the ghostly form of Lady Burlington standing behind her.

CHISWICK HOUSE;
APR-OCT WED-SUN 10-5
www.english-heritage.org.uk/chiswickhouse

9 Leave the house, go clockwise around it, then follow the red gravel path at its rear. Walk through the stone arch to pass between the holly hedges. When you arrive in the gardens keep ahead past the huge stone vases and at the end of the hedge, turn right in front of the greenhouse, veer left on to the path, go right through the brick gateway and then left along the wide path. Turn right out of the gates on to Great West Road and keep ahead until you arrive on the right at Hogarth's House.

At this point, the noise of the traffic becomes a distant murmur. You find yourself in a beautiful garden from which you enter the 'little red-brick house by the Thames' to which satirical

WHERE TO EAT

⑩ THE BLACK LION,
2 South Black Lion Lane;
Tel: 020 8748 2639.
www.massivepub.com
This lovely old pub offers hearty pub meals and excellent beers, as well as a nice garden close to the river.

⑩ THE GEORGE AND DEVONSHIRE,
8 Burlington Gardens;
Tel: 020 8994 1859.
www.georgeanddevonshire.co.uk
This large pub is just a stone's throw away from the Hogarth roundabout. The food on offer ranges from sandwiches to full-blown blow-outs. Service is efficient. A good place to wind down as you near the end of your walk.

artist William Hogarth moved in 1749 and where he spent his declining years. The house contains an exhibition on Hogarth's life and work.

HOGARTH'S HOUSE;
TUE-SUN PM, CLOSED JAN
www.hounslow.info/hogarthshouse

10 Turn right out of Hogarth's House and keep ahead along Hogarth Lane. Bear right on to Burlington Lane and walk to the bus stop. From here you can catch buses travelling towards Hammersmith, or cross to the bus stop on the opposite side of the street for buses travelling towards Richmond.

Mystery in Hampstead

Hampstead is a beautiful village and wandering the wild expanse of the heath is exhilarating. But there is murder – and romance – in the streets.

Much of the first section of this walk will be spent on the heath, but before you start you will visit the pub outside which Ruth Ellis shot dead her lover in 1955 and entered the history books as the last woman to be executed in Britain. There follows an uphill trudge to one of London's finest viewpoints, Parliament Hill, where the skyline unfolds before you. Via the banks of a haunted bathing pool, you then step into a lovely, leafy grove to pay a visit to the house where John Keats wrote *Ode to a Nightingale* and fell in love with the girl next door. Having twisted your way through some of Hampstead's most attractive streets, you come to the grand old house where Daphne du Maurier spent some of her childhood. The walk ends outside an eccentric-looking property that was immortalized as Admiral Boom's house in *Mary Poppins*. As you make your way towards Hampstead Underground Station, be sure to stop off at the Holly Bush tavern to soak up the atmosphere of this wonderful gaslit old hostelry.

Come out of Hampstead Heath railway station, turn right along South Field Park and pause a little way along on the left, outside The Magdala.

This pub blazed into national notoriety on Easter Sunday 1955 when Ruth Ellis arrived here armed with a .38-calibre revolver to confront her estranged lover, David Blakely. He emerged from the pub at around 9.30pm and, as he headed over to his car, Ruth called out to him, but he either didn't hear her or else he ignored her. Raising the gun she shot him and then pursued him round the car firing a second shot. As Blakely fell on to the pavement Ruth Ellis stood over him and fired four more bullets into his body. Other drinkers came out of the pub to see what had happened and Ruth was arrested by an off-duty policeman. At her subsequent trial the defence plea of manslaughter was rendered worthless when she told the court: "It is obvious that when I shot him I intended to kill him." Convicted of murder, she was hanged on 13 July 1955 – the last woman to be executed in Britain. Opinion is still divided over whether Ruth Ellis was a cold calculating murderer or simply suffering from battered woman syndrome – as David Blakely was, without doubt, an unstable drunk who had violently abused her. Regulars at the pub still point out two marks on the outer glazed tiling, just past the first door, as bullet holes from that night long ago, although some people claim they are nothing to do with the shooting. A full article about the murder can be read on the wall inside.

WHERE TO EAT

IOI THE MAGDALA,
2a South Hill Park;
Tel: 020 7435 2503.
Fortify yourself with a bite to eat at the start of the walk.

IOI FREEMASONS ARMS,
32 Downshire Hill;
Tel: 020 7433 6811.
www.freemasonsarms.co.uk
This large, attractive pub has a massive outdoor seating area. The food ranges from burgers to pizzas and steaks.

IOI THE HOLLY BUSH,
22 Holly Mount;
Tel: 020 7435 2892.
Lit by original gaslights, the Holly Bush could be described as the pub that time forgot. Good selection of wines and beers and a variety of meals on offer.

2 Turn left out of the Magdala, go over South Field Park and keep ahead along Parliament Hill. The turning on the right by the red post box is Tanza Road, where at No. 29, a little way along on the left, David Blakely was living with friends at the time of his murder. Keep ahead up Parliament Hill, at the end of which go through the fence on to Hampstead Heath. Ascend the earth path to the right of the information board then go right along the red asphalt path. A little way along you come to the

DISTANCE **4 miles (6.4km)**

ALLOW **2 hours 30 minutes**

START **Hampstead Heath Railway Station, South Field Park Exit**

FINISH **Hampstead Underground Station**

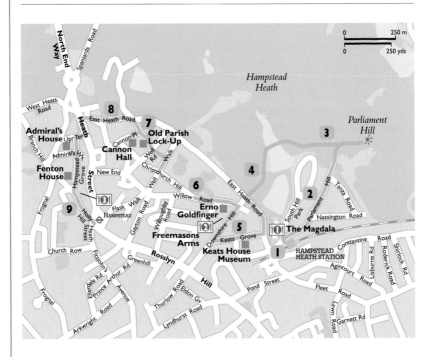

silver information board located on the summit of Parliament Hill.

Once known as Traitor's Hill, there are several explanations as to how this renowned beauty spot acquired its parliamentary association. The most often quoted is that the Gunpowder Conspirators had planned to gather here and watch the destruction of Parliament in 1605. Another explanation is that it was used a defensive position by Parliamentary troops during the English

Civil War. Whatever the origins of its name, the view from here across the London skyline is truly awe-inspiring.

3 Backtrack along the red asphalt path, follow it as it bears right and descends, and just keep going straight until the path veers sharp left and passes between two ponds.

To your right is the mixed bathing area into which hardy swimmers plunge in all weathers. Several have heard footsteps

following close behind them as they prepare to leap into the waters, but on turning they find nobody there. There have been suggestions that the phantom footsteps might be connected with several suicides in the ponds in the distant past.

4 On the other side of the ponds follow the path as it bends sharp left and go right at the next path divide. Keep ahead and cross East Heath Road by the zebra crossing to the right, off which bear left and keep ahead over Downshire Hill, then go next right into Keats Grove. A little way along on the left is Keats House.

The poet John Keats lived here from 1818 to 1820, a period of immense happiness for him. He fell deeply in love with Fanny Brawne, his next-door neighbour's 18-year-old daughter, and the garden's birdsong inspired his best-known poem, *Ode to a Nightingale*. But one February night in 1820 he travelled back to Hampstead on the late coach from London, became feverish and began coughing up drops of blood, the first signs of tuberculosis. On 13 September he left the house and a tearful Fanny Brawne, and set off for the warmer climate of Italy where he died aged just 25. The house is now a museum to his memory and that of his love for the girl next door.

KEATS HOUSE; TUE-SUN, BANK HOLS 1-5; www.cityoflondon.gov.uk/keats

5 Leave the house, go left along Keats Grove, right on to Downshire Hill,

and turn first left into Willow Road and a little way along this road, on the left, pause outside No. 2.

The former home of architect Erno Goldfinger is now owned by the National Trust and is an example of a modernist house that was actually lived in by the designer and his family. Goldfinger also designed much of the furniture and the house contains art works by Henry Moore and Max Ernst. Goldfinger's Modernist style aroused deep and divided emotions, not least in Ian Fleming who used the architect's name as the principal villain in his book *Goldfinger*.

LIMITED OPENING; SEE WEBSITE FOR DETAILS www.nationaltrust.org.uk

6 Continue along Willow Road and, when the road divides at the horse trough, take the right fork up Christchurch Hill and go right on to Well Walk. A history of the Hampstead Spa, established here in the 18th century, can be read on the wall of the Well Tavern on the corner. Head along Well Walk – No. 40 has a blue plaque on the wall to the artist John Constable (1770-1837). A little way past it cross the road, go up the steps by the Chalybeate Well and keep ahead up Well Passage. Cross over Well Road, then veer right and ahead into Cannon Lane where a little way up on the left, at No. 11, is the Old Parish Lock-Up.

This lock-up dates from the 1730s when it was built into the garden wall of Cannon Hall, home of the local Justice of the Peace. The single cell was used as a temporary holding place for wrongdoers who had appeared before him while they were waiting to be transferred to a suitable prison.

7 Keep ahead along Cannon Lane and go left into Cannon Place where, immediately on the left, is Cannon Hall.

Dating from the 18th century, Cannon Hall was the home of Sir Gerald du Maurier (1873-1934) from 1916 until his death. A renowned actor-manager, du Maurier was famed for his inspired interpretations of the works of J M Barrie. He played Captain Hook in the premier production of *Peter Pan*. He was also the father of novelist Daphne du Maurier (1907-1989), who spent much of her childhood here.

8 With your back to the blue plaque on Cannon Hall go diagonally right over the road and keep ahead through Squire's Mount, at the end of which go left along East Heath Road. Cross at the traffic lights and go left along Heath Street. Take the first right into Upper Terrace, go left along Hampstead Grove and first right into Admiral Walk, where a little way along on the right is Admiral's House.

This property owes its eccentric appearance to the tenure of Lt Fountain North, who lived here from 1791 until his death in 1811. It was he who constructed the ship's quarter-deck on the roof that is the house's most striking

feature. Its original owner Admiral Barton is reputed to have fired cannons from the roof to celebrate royal birthdays, a tradition that later led author P L Travers to base Admiral Boom's house in *Mary Poppins* on the property.

9 Backtrack and go right along Hampstead Grove, passing the National Trust's Fenton House on the right, which if it is open is well worth a visit. This section of the walk has a moody ambience that could best be described as urban rustic. Keep ahead down Holly Hill to cross Heath Street via the traffic lights and arrive at Hampstead Station where the walk ends.
FENTON HOUSE; LIMITED OPENING;
SEE WEBSITE www.nationaltrust.org.uk

INDEX

Adelphi Theatre 55
Admiral's House 173
Alfege, St 141
All-Hallows-by-the-Tower 127
Amen Court 94–6
Anne, Queen 43, 93
Apostles 163
Astor Estate Office 71

Baker Street 22, 27
Banqueting House 41
Barbers' Hall 107
Barnes Common 148–53
Belgravia 8–13
Bell Yard 75
Bentham, Jeremy 56, 61
Berkeley Square 33
Big Ben 37
Binnie, Captain Ralph 131
Birdcage Walk 43
Black Lion Lane, Chiswick 163
Blackfriars 92
Bleeding Heart Yard 83
Bligh, Captain 120, 124
Bolan, Marc 148, 149
Boleyn, Anne 154, 159
Bridewell 40–1
Britton, Thomas 79–80
Buckingham Palace 15, 43, 44
Burlington Arms 166
Burton, Sir Richard 153

Cabinet War Rooms 36, 41
Cable Street 120, 121
Cannon Hall 173
Castle Pub 79
Cato Street 14, 19
Cecil Court 54
Chapel Street 12–13
Chapman, Annie 112, 117
Charles I, King 36, 37, 41, 42,
    44, 47, 144
Charles II, King 47, 144, 163

Charlotte, Queen 60
Charterhouse Square 85
Chesterfield Street 30
Chiswick 162–7
Chiswick House 162, 166–7
Christ Church Spitalfields 117
Christchurch Greyfriars 96
Church of the Immaculate
    Conception 32
Church Street Causeway 164
Churchill, Winston 36, 41
Cleopatra's Needle 64, 68–9
Clerkenwell 78–83
Clerks Well 83
Clermont Club 32–3
Clink Prison 134, 138
Cockpit Steps 43
Collins, Wilkie 14, 16–18
Covent Garden 64–9
Crewe House 29–30
Criterion Brasserie 51
Cromwell, Oliver 37, 68, 110,
    155, 166
Cross Bones Graveyard 135–6
Crutched Friars 130
Cutty Sark 140, 145

The Da Vinci Code 70, 74
Dadd, Richard 51
Dee, Dr John 103
Diana, Princess 44
Dickens, Charles 51, 57, 70, 78,
    83, 130, 134, 135
Downing Street 36, 41
Doyle, Sir Arthur Conan 13,
    22, 26
Druitt, Montague John 72–4,
    163, 164, 166
Drury Lane Gardens 65
du Maurier, Daphne 168, 173

Ebury Street 9
Eddowes, Catherine 112,

    113–14
Ellis, Ruth 168, 169
Epstein, Brian 8, 12–13

Fan Museum 141, 142
Fawkes, Guy 38
Ferryman's Seat 138
Fleming, Ian 9

Garrick Theatre 52–4
The George 75
George, Prince Regent 79
George Street 16–18
The Globe (pub) 60
Globe Theatre 134, 136–8
Golden Hinde 139
Goldfinger, Erno 172
Goldsmith, Oliver 74
Goodwin's Court 54
Gray's Antiques Market 23
Great Fire 84, 86, 88, 89, 126,
    127
Green Street 15
Greenwich 140–5
Grey, Lady Jane 85, 110–11
Groom Place 10–12
Guildhall 110–11
Guildhall Art Gallery 111
Gunpowder Plot 38, 170

Ham House 154, 159
Hampstead 168–73
Hanbury Street 117
Handel, George Frideric 23, 80
Hatton, Lady Elizabeth 83
Hen and Chickens Court 75
Hendrix, Jimi 22
Henry VIII, King 154, 155,
    158–9
Hill, Octavia 135
Hoesch, Leopold von 46–7
Hogarth, William 41, 58, 166,
    167

Hogarth's House 162, 167
Holmes, Sherlock 22, 26, 27, 42, 47, 50, 51
Horse Guards 41
Houses of Parliament 36, 37
Hunterian Museum 57–8

In and Out Club 29
Inner Temple 70, 72
Inns of Court 71
Isabella, Queen 92, 96

Jack the Ripper 70, 72–4, 112–17, 162, 163
Jewel Tower 38

Keats, John 168, 172
Keeler, Christine 26
Kelly, Mary 112, 117
Kent, William 33
KGB 32
Kidd, Captain William 125
King's Bench Walk 72
Köningsmark, Count 46

Lamb and Flag pub 54–5
Langtry, Lillie 15
Leadenhall Market 130
Lincoln's Inn Fields 58
Lindsey House 57
London Stone 98, 103
London Wall 107, 108–10
Lord North Street 40
Lord Raglan pub 97
Lovatt, Lord 127
Lucan, Lord 8, 9–10
Lyceum Theatre 68

Manchester Street 26–7
Marble Arch 14, 15
Marshalsea Prison 135
Mayfair 28–33
Middle Temple 70, 71
Middlesex Sessions House 82
Milbourne House 152
Milton, John 106, 110

Mount Street Garden 32
Museum of London 106

Nash, John 15, 43, 51
Nelson, Lord 52, 68
Newgate Prison 89, 96, 107
Nichols, Mary 112, 116
Nightingale, Florence 139
North Row Buildings 15

Old Cemetery (Barnes) 152
Old Cock Tavern 74
Old Curiosity Shop 57
Old Operating Theatre 139
Old Parish Lock Up 172–3
Orton, Arthur 18–19
Orwell, George 56, 60
Over, John 139

Paddington Street Gardens 26
Parliament Hill 168, 170
Peasants Revolt 88
Pepys, Samuel 65, 126, 127, 128
Petrie Museum 61
Piccadilly 28, 29
Pickering Place 46
Plague 65, 85, 108
Plumber's Arms 9
Postman's Park 96–7
Princelet Street 116–17
Priory of the Dominicans 93
Priory of St Elsing Spital 110
Profumo affair 22, 26
Prospect of Whitby 125
Pump Court 71–2

Queen Anne's Gate 42, 43
Queen's House 140, 144
Queen's Larder 60

Rahere 88
Ranger's House 140, 141–2
Red Cross Garden 135
Richmond Palace 155
Richmond Park 154–9

River Police 125
Roman Bath 68
Roman Temple 102
Royal Naval College 140, 144–5
Royal Observatory 140, 144

Saddlers Hall 97
St Alfege 108, 140, 141
St Alphage Garden 108–10
St Andrew By The Wardrobe 93
St Bartholomew the Great 86–8
St Bride's 89
St Clement Danes Church 75
St Dunstan in the West 75
St George-in-the-East 121
St George's Burial Ground 26
St Giles Cripplegate 107–8, 110
St James Garlickhythe 102
St James's 42–7
St James's Church 80–2
St James's Palace 42, 44
St James's Park 42, 43
St James's Square 46
St John's Ambulance 79
St Martin-in-the-Fields 50, 52, 65
St Mary le Bow 99
St Mary Magdalen 153
St Michael Paternoster Royal 103
St Michael's Alley 130–1
St Nicholas, Chiswick 166
St Olave's 128
St Paul's Cathedral 92, 93–4, 98, 100
St Paul's Covent Garden 50
St Peter upon Cornhill 130
St Sepulchre's Church 89
St Thomas's hospital 139
Seething Lane 128
Senate House 60
Shakespeare, William 71, 78,

79, 92, 93, 99, 134, 136–9
Shepherd Market 28, 29
Smithfield Meat Market 86
Soane, Sir John 56, 58–60
Somerset House 64, 68
Southcott, Joanna 27
Southwark Cathedral 139
Spencer Hotel 15–16
Spiritualist Association 13
Spring Heeled Jack 148, 150–2
Steinberg, Ellen 80–2
Stoker, Bram 64, 68
Sweeney Todd 70, 75

Temple Bar 94
Temple Church 70, 74
Terriss, William 55
Texan Republic 46
Thames, River 71, 138, 152, 164
Theatre Royal, Drury Lane 65
Theatre Royal Haymarket 51

Thynne, Thomas 46
Tichborne Claimant 18–19
Tobacco Dock 120, 122–4
Tower of London 126, 154, 159
Trafalgar Square 50, 52
Turner, Joseph 120, 124, 158
Turpin, Dick 148, 149, 166
Tyburn 15, 85, 107

United Friends Synagogue 117
University College London 61

Vancouver, George 159
Viaduct Tavern 88–9
Villiers, Barbara 163–4

Wallace, Sir William 88
Wallace Collection 27
Walpole House 163
Wapping 120–5
Wapping Old Stairs 125

Ward, Dr Stephen 26
Wellington, Duke of 13
Wernher Collection 141–2
Westminster 36–41
Westminster Abbey 36, 40
Westminster School 40
Whitechapel 112–17
Whitehall Palace 36, 41
Whittington, Dick 98, 99, 103
Wilde, Jonathan 57–8
William III, King 46, 99–100
Williams, John 121–2
Williamson's Tavern 99–100
Willow Road 172
Wilton Row 13
Wimpole Mews 23–6
Wimpole Street 26
Wren, Sir Christopher 72, 89, 98, 99, 100, 102

York, Frederic, Duke of 42, 45
York Watergate 69

ACKNOWLEDGEMENTS

The Automobile Association wishes to thank the following photographers, companies and picture libraries for their assistance in the preparation of this book.

Abbreviations for the picture credits are as follows – (AA) AA World Travel Library

3 AA/R Mort; 6/7 AA; 8 AA/R Harris; 11 Richard Jones; 12 Richard Jones; 13 Pictures Colour Library; 14 AA/M Jourdan; 17 AA/M Jourdan; 18 Richard Jones; 20/21 GettyImages; 22 Pictures Colour Library; 23 Handel House Museum/Matthew Hollow; 25 Pictures Colour Library; 28 AA/R Turpin; 29 Alamy (© Andrew Holt); 31 AA/R Turpin; 32 Alamy (© Michael Jenner); 34/35 AA/B Smith; 36 AA/J A Tims; 39 AA/J A Tims; 42 AA/R Turpin; 43 AA/T Woodcock; 45 Richard Jones; 47 AA/M Trelawney; 48/49 Alamy (© Arco Images); 50 Pictures Colour Library; 51 AA/J A Tims; 53 Pictures Colour Library; 54 Pictures Colour Library; 56 AA/M Trelawney; 59 AA/M Trelawney; 61 Alamy (© Dominic Burke); 62/63 AA/M Jourdan; 64 AA/S McBride; 67 AA/M Jourdan; 69 AA/P Kenward; 70 AA/P Wilson; 73 AA/R Strange; 74 Alamy (© Mark Lucas); 76/77 AA; 78 Pictures Colour Library; 79 Pictures Colour Library; 81 Pictures Colour Library; 82 AA/W Voysey; 84 Alamy (© David Willis); 87 AA/P Kenward; 89 Pictures Colour Library; 90/91 AA/M Trelawney; 92 Pictures Colour Library; 93 Alamy (© Michael Jenner); 95 AA/R Strange; 96 Alamy (© Martyn Vickery); 98 AA/R Victor; 99 AA/R Victor; 101 Alamy (© Paul Debois); 102 AA/R Strange; 104/105 AA/R Turpin; 106 Richard Jones; 109 AA/T Woodcock; 111 AA/J A Tims; 112 Alamy (© Andrew Holt); 113 Pictures Colour Library; 115 AA/R Turpin; 116 AA/J A Tims; 118/119 Alamy (© Holmes Garden Photos); 120 Alamy (© Magwitch); 121 Richard Jones; 123 AA/B Smith; 125 Pictures Colour Library; 126 AA; 129 AA/P Kenward; 131 AA/R Turpin; 132/133 AA/S McBride; 134 AA/M Jourdan; 137 AA/R Turpin; 138 AA/S McBride; 140 AA/P Kenward; 143 Pictures Colour Library; 145 AA/N Setchfield; 146/147 AA/N Setchfield; 148 AA/G Wrona; 151 Richard Jones; 153 Richard Jones; 154 Richard Jones; 157 AA/M Trelawney; 160/161 AA/S & O Mathews; 162 Pictures Colour Library; 165 AA/M Trelawney; 168 AA/J Tims; 171 Pictures Colour Library; 173 AA/M Trelawney

Every effort has been made to trace the copyright holders, and we apologise in advance for any unintentional omissions or errors. We would be please to apply any corrections in any following edition of this publication.